赞比亚农业发展及其对小农生计的影响

Assessment of the Status
of the Zambia's Agriculture Sector Development Framework and
Its Impacts and
Contribution to Improvement of Small Scale
Producers' Livelihoods

卢萨卡国际消费者团结与信托协会　著
Customer Unity and Trust Society- International Lusaka

刘海方　田　欣　周灿灿　译

社会科学文献出版社
SOCIAL SCIENCES ACADEMIC PRESS (CHINA)

ACF	Agriculture Consultative Forum，农业咨询论坛
CAADP	Comprehensive African Agriculture Development Programme，非洲农业发展综合计划
CBOs	Community Based Organisations，社区组织
CSO	Central Statistics Office，中央统计办公室
CUTS	Consumer Unity and Trust Society，消费者团结与信托协会
DACO	District Agriculture Coordinator，地方农业协调员
FAO	Food and Agriculture Organisation，联合国粮食及农业组织
FISP	Farmers Input Support Programme，农民投入支持项目
FRA	Food Reserve Agency，粮食储备署
FSRP	Food Security Research Project，粮食安全研究项目
GDP	Gross Domestic Product，国内生产总值
IFAD	International Fund for Agriculture Development，国际农业发展基金会
MAL	Ministry of Agriculture and Livestock，农牧业部
NGOs	Non Governmental Organisations，非政府组织
NISIR	National Institute of Scientific and Industrial Research，国家科学与工业研究院
NSTC	National Science and Technology Council，国家科学技术委员会
SCCI	Seed Control and Certification Institute，种子管理与认证协会
SNDP	Sixth National Development Plan，第六个国家发展计划
TSB	Technical Service Branch，技术服务司
UNCTAD	United Nation Conference on Trade and Development，联合国贸易和发展会议
UNDP	United Nations Development Programme，联合国开发计划署
ZEMA	Zambia Environmental Management Agency，赞比亚环境管理署
ZDA	Zambia Development Agency，赞比亚发展署
ZDHS	Zambia Demographic and Health Survey，赞比亚人口与健康调查

概　要

赞比亚政府和其他利益相关方为建立一个有利的环境，帮助农民从小生产者逐渐成长为中等规模生产者而实施了各种项目和计划，然而现实与这个目标仍相距甚远。不可否认，农业是赞比亚经济的支柱产业，这就意味着农业增长是赞比亚实现减贫最为清晰的路径。众所周知，农业和减贫关系密不可分，但近十多年来对农业领域的公共投资仍然匮乏。公共投资不足所带来的种种制约对小农生产者产生了极大的影响，抑制了他们实现商品化生产的能力。本研究旨在评估赞比亚农业发展框架（Zambia's Agriculture Sector Development Framework）是否足以提供使小农生产者改善生计、成长为中等规模生产者的条件。

研究结果表明，赞比亚拥有丰富的土地、劳动力和水资源，农业生产潜力巨大。赞比亚有7500万公顷土地，其中58%的土地所处地区的年降雨量可达800～1400毫米，属中、上等农业用地。同样，赞比亚的土地状况适宜种植多种作物，以及发展渔业和畜牧业。据联合国粮食及农业组织（FAO）估计，目前赞比亚农业用地的利用率仅为14%。

尽管农业有巨大的发展潜力，但赞比亚农民目前仍面临许多挑战，这些挑战包括难以获得承担得起的信贷、农业推广服务、兽医服务、便利的物资运输和存储设施，并且缺乏一个完善的市场。有充足的证据表明，受到这些制约影响最大的是从事小规模生产的农民。事实上，70%的赞比亚农民是小规模生产者，主导了玉米、小米、高粱、花生和棉花等农作物的生产，在降水充沛、土地肥沃等有利条件下，他们有更多机会参与到农业增长计划中来。农业有潜力在赞比亚的经济增长中发挥更大的促进作用。然而遗憾的是，即使目前有数项政府和捐赠者资助的项目，小农还是未能成长为中等规模生产者，造成这一现状的原因在于刺激小农生产发展的主要因素仍旧处于落后状态。

本研究报告指出，目前赞比亚农业仍有较大的发展空间，特别是如果能给予小农更多的关注，因为小农占到了赞比亚农民总数的70%，几乎主导了玉米、小米、高粱、花生和棉花等作物的种植。报告同时也列出了一些亟待关注的问题，这些问题的解决有助于提高农民的生活水平。虽然现行政策已注意到这些问题，但解决问题的措施仍未到位。

赞比亚的农业发展构架以国家农业政策（National Agriculture Policy, NAP）为指导。国家农业政策为农业发展提供了框架，规定了赞比亚发展农业的一些基本原则。所以分析这项政策对于本研究而言至关重要。例如，国家农业政策规定，要通过对种子进行实验、检验、品种登记、品种保护、实施种子质量标准来规范种子产业，以推动种子贸易、检疫和其他与种子相关事业的发展。虽然棉农们均使用了（经过国家检验的）优质棉花种子，但花生生产领域仍面临着一些问题，因为农民还是使用着（自家地里生产的）回收种子。国家农业政策为推动种子部门的发展，规定直接由研究机构向种子生产部门提供种畜和原种种子，调查结果显示，由于缺乏分拣技术，种植花生的农民无法分出花生的品种和等级。

国家农业政策也提出赞比亚需要一个有效的农业推广和信息交换系统。然而本报告也指出，在充足的人员配置和运作效率方面，尚需要进行能力建设，也应该使得推广服务更容易获得。这就需要每方圆10千米即设置一个地方农业协调员（DACO）的下级分支办公点。

国家农业政策意识到有必要成立一个基金以鼓励集体贷款，但迄今尚未解决获取农业资助方面的问题。因此，本报告建议政府应该通过合作系统促进小额信贷的供应，也应鼓励农民建立自助团体。

此外，虽然国家农业政策承诺采取措施推动市场信息在不同地区的利益相关者间流动，包括促进农村基础设施（如道路、农村仓储设施等）的建设以及发展市场中心，但对从事小规模生产的农民而言，市场仍是一个挑战。因此，国家农业政策在市场领域的政策亟须贯彻执行。

在灌溉方面，政策执行不力同样明显。既定的策略包括了提升灌溉工程的规划、设计、建设的标准和指导水平，以使从事小规模生产的农民受惠，但这仍未大规模开展。本报告建议，如果农民能够使用多种替代的灌溉手段（如安装水泵），能够保证雨水资源的供给和存储，并且利益相关方能在基层实施适宜的管理计划，那么小农的生产能力就会得到提高。

这项研究关注的另一项政策是合作发展政策（Cooperative Development Policy），也就是为改善小规模生产农户的绩效而制定的相关策略。具体而言，就是通过构建一个法律和制度框架，促进合作组织的重新定位与改革；同时确保负责合作事宜的部门能够在所有地区派驻基层工作人员，直接出面处理合作问题，本课题组的研究认为这是一项积极的政策建议。为保证农民们获得生产回报，应进一步鼓励合作农业的发展。

本研究关注的一个具体农业产业是山羊的养殖和贸易。研究发现，养羊农户主要面临转变观念的问题：现实中人们采用随意散养的方法，而不是正规集群饲养，要使山羊养殖成为主流产业，需要转变这样的养殖观念。肉牛生产也是如此。所以，当务之急是观念引导和小农的生产能力建设，使得他们将牛羊的养殖作为额外收入的获取途径，以便在家庭和社区层面能够再投资于社会和经济方面。

研究还证实，尽管在农业领域的投资受到欢迎，但也有一些需要注意的问题，以保证投资符合"负责任农业投资原则"（The Principles of Responsible Agricultural Investments，PRAI）。农民对土地及相关自然资源的所有权应当得到认可和尊重，保证当事的农户不会在违背其意愿的情况下失去土地。本研究也建议，作为对土地所有权的尊重，应该确保农民在获得土地时掌握全部相关信息。研究进一步发现，在新投资地区，被迁移的农民重新获得土地的可能性较低，这意味着投资可能会危及粮食安全，因为产量会低于投资前的情况。

最后，本研究还指出了脆弱的土地所有权制度将会给农民带来的问题。报告指出，赞比亚土地所有权的主要形式是传统的土地所有制。只有 37.5% 的受访者表示他们拥有地契，其中约 70% 来自铜带省，该省是一个以城市为主的省份。拥有地契将会极大地帮助农民从金融机构获得贷款，因为地契可以被用作融资的担保物。

目 录

1. 背景 / 1
   1.1 问题陈述 / 2
   1.2 研究原理 / 2
   1.3 研究目标 / 2
   1.4 方法 / 3

2. 赞比亚农业部门概况 / 6
   2.1 农业部门的发展变迁 / 7
   2.2 小农户的参与 / 8
      2.2.1 参与关键性农业活动 / 8
      2.2.2 小农对生产的贡献 / 8
      2.2.3 性别动因 / 9
   2.3 关键性成果指标 / 10
      2.3.1 农业对国民收入的贡献 / 10
      2.3.2 农业对减贫的贡献 / 11
      2.3.3 农业对粮食安全和营养状况的贡献 / 12

3. 提高小规模生产的政策和制度体系 / 14
   3.1 政策体系 / 14
      3.1.1 国家农业政策（2004~2015）/ 14
      3.1.2 灌溉政策（2004）/ 17

3.1.3　国家种子产业政策（1999）/ 19
　　　3.1.4　国家合作发展政策（2011）/ 21
　　3.2　组织机构 / 23
　　3.3　实施策略 / 24

4. 农业投资 / 27

5. 实地调查发现 / 33
　　5.1　投入 / 33
　　　5.1.1　土地 / 33
　　　5.1.2　灌溉 / 34
　　　5.1.3　获得推广服务/投入 / 35
　　　5.1.4　获得贷款 / 37
　　　5.1.5　获得兽医服务 / 37
　　　5.1.6　能否使用到最就近的永久道路 / 39
　　5.2　产出端 / 40
　　5.3　营销问题 / 41

6. 总结与建议 / 44

参考文献 / 47

附件　《赞比亚农业发展及其对小农生计的影响》英文 / 49

1 背　景

农业部门是赞比亚所有经济部门中的重中之重，是赞比亚实现经济可持续发展的杠杆和指标。该部门责任重大，因为赞比亚大多数经济问题都直接或间接与这一部门的表现相关。从经济和社会发展到粮食安全，农业具有多种功能，这些功能主要通过换取外汇、农村发展和减贫的方式实现。最近的数据显示：赞比亚农业发展迟缓，其增长率约为4%，低于非洲农业发展综合计划（CAADP）建议的6%的增长率。[①] 与2003年的《马普托宣言》（Maputo Declaration）一样，非洲农业发展综合计划要求非洲各国政府将至少10%的国家预算投入农业部门，以实现年增长至少6%的目标。尽管不够发达，农业仍是赞比亚需要劳动力最集中的产业，全国超过70%的劳动力从事农业，80%以上的人口生活在农村地区并依赖农业为生。农业对国内生产总值的贡献约为21%，落后于服务业和采掘行业。[②] 赞比亚的国家政策和发展体系都将农业视为一个潜在的经济驱动力。

为使赞比亚农业部门能有效实现其目标，必须将重点放在小农和小生产者上，因为他们占据了人口的多数并持续贫困。改进小规模农业生产体系至关重要，改进工作应当通过多种方式进行，包括建立全新的创新型公私伙伴关系，增加对提高生产力相关领域的研究和推广系统的公私投资，以及推动

---

① 《赞比亚人类发展报告》，联合国开发计划署，2011。
② 《国家合作发展政策（2011）》，赞比亚农牧业部，2011。

以发展为导向的地方治理和机构设置等。此外，解决其他限制农业发展的普遍问题，如灌溉、水源、生产能力、生产效率、储存、市场情报和准入、运输系统等，对于推进农业部门发展而言也是必要的。所有这些都是赞比亚农业发展综合计划的重要组成部分。因此，这项研究具有重要意义，目标是评估赞比亚发展体系在多大程度上帮助小农户和小生产者改善了他们的生活。

1.1 问题陈述

由于农业是赞比亚农村经济的支柱，农业的增长显然是赞比亚减贫的最有效途径。尽管一般认为农业发展与减贫之间的关系密不可分，但在过去的十多年里，农业领域的公共投资依旧持续不足，从事小规模生产的农民仍长期在贫困中挣扎。赞比亚的首要政策目标是加速农业发展，增强农业竞争力，但除非保障在这一领域有充足的公共资源投入，否则这一目标便不能实现。公共投入如果能够长期进入研发领域、推广服务部门、农村基础设施建设领域和粮食安全与质量系统，收效就非常显著，这是促进农业增长、提升其竞争力的最重要驱动力。多数情况下，从事小规模生产的农民受到农业生产商品化制约因素的影响很大。在这种情况下，有必要了解赞比亚的农业发展体系在何种程度上帮助小农户和小生产者促进了生产，并最终改善其生计。

1.2 研究原理

赞比亚农业生产主要以农村地区小规模生产的农户为主，他们在全面参与赞比亚农业增长体系时面临着各种不同的障碍。尽管政府和非政府组织提出并实施了多种方案，以便创造有利的环境，促使从事小规模农业生产的农民转变为中等规模的生产者（就其产量和生产效率而言），但这个目标迄今还与现实距离甚远。本研究的重要意义就在于此，即评估赞比亚农业发展体系是否足够有用、有效，同时也为改善这一体系提出了建议。

1.3 研究目标

这项研究的目标包括以下内容：

- 考察赞比亚农业发展体系的政策、发展的性质、如何支持减贫、关键部门、公共和私人投资的水平等；
- 考察哪些政策对小农，尤其是妇女造成负面影响；
- 研究分析小规模生产者的参与和作用，考察农业在减贫方面的作用及性质、规模和程度，对从事农业的妇女给予特别的关注；
- 分析小农参与增长体系的特殊机遇，确定哪些因素阻碍了他们的全面参与；
- 对良好的公私伙伴关系的概貌进行研究，分析其实践和政策，以及贫困农民如何参与评估这些伙伴关系；考察可能对改善生计和减贫更为有效的替代性或潜在的投资领域；
- 评估现行的农业发展体系对贫困的农民社区产生的直接和长期影响，具体的评估应当从市场准入、服务、资源和对粮食作物的种植的影响等方面来进行；
- 比照既已确定的目标——如非洲农业发展综合计划——来评价农业部门的实际表现。

1.4 方法

本研究从三个阶段，即投入、产出和市场对农业次级市场进行了评估，其具体定义如下。

- 投入：主要包括获取信贷、种子、肥料和水源或灌溉的相关问题（公共和私人投资如何发挥作用）；推广服务（服务设施的效率和功能如何）；获得优质饲料、优质牧草和水源；获得及时优质的兽医服务等。
- 产出：主要包括收割后保鲜贮藏设施、交通基础设施、市场营销和类似的市场营销机构等。
- 市场：主要包括特定产品能否进入市场；小农能否获得市场信息；供应方面现存的无竞争力的现状及其应对等。

本研究选择了三种作物进行详细的分析。选择的标准是：第一，就种植面积而言该作物是主要作物；第二，该作物的种植以小农为主导，因为本研究旨在改善小农的生计状况。基于《2011/2012年度农产品收成预测》结果，筛选出的作物分别是玉米、棉花和花生。为进行更为全面的评估，本研究还选取了山羊和肉牛的养殖进行研究，因为这两种牲畜在小农的畜牧养殖中占有最重要的地位。

为了评估是否存在更有效地改善农民生计的可替代性的或潜在的投资区域，消费者团结与信托协会（CUTS）对农业部门多年来接受的外来投资进行了评估。尤其是，这项评估充分考虑到了外国和本地投资进入三种作物和牲畜的生产养殖的三个阶段。这项评估所依据的原则是由联合国粮农组织、国际农业发展基金会（IFAD）、联合国贸易和发展会议（UNCTAD）和世界银行（World Bank, WB）共同制定的"负责任农业投资原则"，具体与本评估相关的原则包括以下内容。

- 原则一：承认和尊重既存的对土地及其相关自然资源的权利。
- 原则二：投资不会危及粮食安全而会加强粮食安全。
- 原则三：在一个适合的商业、法律和监管环境下，农业投资相关的过程是透明的、受监督的，并确保涉及所有利益相关者的问责制度。
- 原则四：向所有实际受影响者征询意见，记录咨询后达成的协议，并予以落实。
- 原则五：投资者在实施投资项目时必须遵守法律，体现行业最佳操作实践，在经济上切实可行，并产生持久的共同价值。
- 原则六：投资产生良好的社会和分配效益，避免增加风险。
- 原则七：量化项目对环境的影响，采取措施鼓励资源的可持续利用，同时尽量使负面影响的风险最小化，如果负面影响不可避免，要予以减轻。

本报告通过分析二手资料和原始资料解析上述问题，具体如下。

二手资料分析

这涉及对可用的政策及政策在决策和实施层面上的协同配合进行评估，评价这些政策是否足以在价值链中的三个阶段促进农业的发展。国家农业政策与其他次级市场政策构成了分析的基础。

原始资料

为了掌握第一手信息，本研究还使用了原始资料。原始资料的收集既包括通过设计结构性问题从关键人士那里收集信息，也包括对选定的样本发放结构性调查问卷。前一种方式主要用于采访在与农业发展相关的关键机构里任职的高级官员，这些机构包括地方农业协调员办公室、农业咨询论坛（ACF）、畜牧业发展信托基金（Livestock Development Trust）、地方农业政策研究所（Indaba Agricultural Policy Research Institute）、赞比亚全国农民协会（ZNFU）、赞比亚肉牛协会（Beef Association of Zambia）、赞比亚发展署（ZDA）和赞比亚棉花协会（Cotton Association of Zambia）。

为了深入了解城镇和地区的真实情况，有必要设计问卷调查。本研究对120名农民进行了采访，收集了他们的意见和经验。在这120名农民中，40人来自铜带省（Copperbelt Province），40人来自东部省（Eastern Province），40人来自南部省（Southern Province）。南部省具有发展小规模农户牛羊养殖的巨大潜力，但是这种潜力目前仍没有得到充分的开发。铜带省的城镇化水平较高，采矿业是其传统主导产业，但近年来该省的农业发展开始起步。与其他省份相比，东部省主要以小农生产为主，在棉花、花生和玉米的生产方面表现出色，此外，该省的肉牛和山羊养殖也可圈可点。这在《2011/2012年度农产品收成预测》中得到了证实。

数据分析

在实地调查工作结束以后，研究者在一个利益相关者参加的工作坊中分析和展示了收集到的资料和信息。

本研究的局限性

本研究的进行时间相对有限。这意味着几乎没有时间采访不同的利益相关者，也意味着未能对一些重要的利益相关者进行约访。在如何获取可靠信息方面也存在问题，因为有些关键数据并不是由权威机构记录的，例如单项农作物和牲畜对农业在国内生产总值中所占份额的影响。

2 赞比亚农业部门概况

由于赞比亚拥有充足的土地、劳动力和水资源，其在发展农业生产方面拥有极大潜力。赞比亚土地总面积为7500万公顷，鉴于部分地区年降雨量为800~1400毫米，58%的土地可被划归为中、上等土地。赞比亚的土地也适合多种农作物的种植及渔业、畜牧业的发展。据估计，目前被实际利用的土地仅占农业可用地的14%。[1] 在非洲南部国家中，赞比亚是拥有最优地表水和地下水资源的国家之一，拥有众多的河流、湖泊和水坝。此外，赞比亚许多地区丰富的地下含水层为灌溉项目的实施提供了良好的条件，而这些水体多数尚未被开发。虽然这个国家的灌溉潜力保守估计是42.3万公顷，但目前只有5万公顷的土地得到了灌溉，意味着这种资源远未得到充分利用。[2]

依据不同的降水模式，可以将赞比亚划分为三个农业生态区。第一区域的特点是降水少，作物生长期短，生长季节伴随着高温，易发生旱灾。第三区域的特点是降水多，作物生长期长，发生干旱的可能性小，作物生长季节气候凉爽。第二区域因为具有最广泛的气候多样性而介于第一区域和第三区域之间。[3] 这三个区域在农业经济特征方面（降雨、海拔高度、平均温度、植

---

[1] 凯琳达·汤姆森等：《土地利用综合评估数据在赞比亚农林政策评估与分析中的运用》，联合国粮食及农业组织，2008。
[2] 凯琳达·汤姆森等：《土地利用综合评估数据在赞比亚农林政策评估与分析中的运用》，联合国粮食及农业组织，2008。
[3] J. 法林顿、O. 萨萨：《赞比亚农业改革的驱动力：辨析塑造政策环境的因素》，英国国际发展署，2002。

被和土壤）差异很大。第一区域主要分布在赞比亚的山谷地区，如赞比亚东部的卢安瓜山谷和南部的格温贝山谷。西部和南部省的部分地区也属于第一区域。第二区域主要分布在赞比亚的中部地区，即中央省、东部省、卢萨卡省、南部省，还包括西部省的部分地区。第三区域基本上分布在这个国家的北部，包括北部省、卢阿普拉省、铜带省和西北省。

2.1 农业部门的发展变迁

不同时期经济政策的变化，对赞比亚农业部门的发展变迁有着决定性的影响。表1按时间顺序列出了经济政策的变迁情况。这些变化导致了赞比亚农业部门运作方式的演变。在第一个阶段，赞比亚施行管制经济政策，政府为农民提供所有的生产投入、服务和现成的市场。农民在产品的生产与营销方面过度依赖政府。

1991年，赞比亚政府引入了一套完整的结构调整方案，意味着其经济体制从指令型经济转变为自由型经济。这意味着农民们不得不在投入和营销方面依靠自己的力量。这一转变给农民们造成了极大的困难，导致全国农业生产的下降。

2001年，赞比亚政府决定将农业作为首要发展对象，并制定了国家农业政策（2004~2015），这一政策对农业部门的发展起到了促进作用。

表1 赞比亚经济政策变化时间表

1982年12月以前	中央规划和管控体制
1982年12月至1985年10月	放松和解除管制
1985年10月至1987年4月	高度自由化的体制
1987年5月至1988年11月	恢复管制
1988年11月至1989年6月	放松部分管制
1989年7月至1991年11月	走向全面自由化的政策
1991年11月至2001年12月	完整的结构调整方案
2001年12月至今	(a)谨慎的自由化/私有化方式；(b)重新引入国家计划；(c)国家发展计划的发展

资料来源：J.法林顿、O.萨萨：《赞比亚农业改革的驱动力：辨析塑造政策环境的因素》，英国国际发展署，2002。

2.2 小农户的参与

2.2.1 参与关键性农业活动

生活在农村地区的大部分农民都是小农,主要从事勉强维生的基本生产。如果政府在仔细考虑之后推出有利于小农们的相关政策,为他们创造一个有利的环境,帮助他们实现生产的多样化、提高生产力、顺利进入目标市场,就可以实现小农推动农业部门发展的目标。

考虑到赞比亚降雨模式和土壤肥力的有利条件,小农参与农业发展体系的机会和潜力极大。通过增加人均国民生产总值和减轻农村社区的贫困状况,农业能够成为推动赞比亚经济增长的一个更大的动力。尽管赞比亚农民在扩大生产和增加销售上存在着巨大的潜力,但农业部门目前仍处于落后状态。就产量和生产效率而言,政府和捐助者资助的各项计划未能使小农成长为从事中等规模经营的农民,这是由于促进小农生产迅速发展的要素仍然发展缓慢。只有在赞比亚政府设法为小农减小有关投入、培训、推广服务及收获后的管理和市场等方面的压力后,才能实现农业显著的增长。此外,政府还应提供必要的基础设施(修建公路支线等),以降低在农村社区从事农业生产的成本。

2.2.2 小农对生产的贡献

显而易见,在赞比亚从事种植业的主要是小农,占所有农民的比例超过70%。根据《2011/2012年度农产品收成预测》,小农主导了玉米、小米、高粱、花生、棉花等作物的生产,其生产量分别占各项作物生产量的95%、99.9%、93%、99.5%和99.4%。这表明小农对赞比亚整个农业生产作出了巨大的贡献。有关赞比亚的主要作物玉米的考察可以证实这一点。表2表明了大规模农户和小规模农户在玉米产量中所占的份额。

表2 不同类别农民生产的玉米份额

单位：吨,%

年份 玉米产量	2002/2003	2003/2004	2004/2005	2005/2006	2006/2007	2007/2008	2008/2009
大规模农户	412381	253861	254804	313519	287089	218728	229893
小规模农户	745479	959740	611382	1110919	1079069	992838	1657117
总产量	1157861	1213601	866187	1424439	1366158	1211566	1887010
大规模农户的比率	36	21	29	22	21	18	12

资料来源：《第六次赞比亚国家发展计划，2011～2015，公民社会视角（2010）》，赞比亚民间减贫组织，2010。

表2表明，大规模农户生产的玉米产量占玉米总产量的份额不断下降，从2002/2003年度的36%降到了2008/2009年度的12%。这表明小农是支撑赞比亚农业的主要力量，他们对农业的贡献非常重要。

2.2.3 性别动因

农业是赞比亚的主要就业部门，分别有49%的女性和48%的男性从事农业。[①] 然而从事农业的大多数女性（55%）并没有获得劳动报酬。[②] 妇女生产了80%的粮食，妇女也占自给自足的农业生产者的80%。[③] 尽管在农业生产中妇女占据了重要地位，但她们在技术、信贷、推广服务和生产投入等方面受到诸多的限制。农民投入支持项目（FISP）很少涉及女性农民的参与就证实了这一点。为实现农村地区经济增长的最大化和减贫的目标，必须有意识地针对性解决性别问题。

需要认识到，农业是赞比亚的主要就业部门。表3清楚地表明，女性户主家庭的贫困状况持续保持在最高水平上。

---

① 《第六个赞比亚国家发展计划，2011～2015，公民社会视角（2010）》，赞比亚民间减贫组织，2010。
② 《赞比亚人口健康调查》，赞比亚中央统计办公室，2007。
③ 《第六个赞比亚国家发展计划，2011～2015，公民社会视角（2010）》，赞比亚民间减贫组织，2010。

表3　2006年男性户主和女性户主家庭的贫困状况

	绝对贫困（%）	非常贫困（%）	不贫困（%）	人口总数（个）
男性户主	63	49	34	9395704
女性户主	70	57	29	2289327
全　　国	64	51	32	11685031

资料来源：《赞比亚人类发展报告》，联合国开发计划署，2011。

2.3　关键性成果指标

2.3.1　农业对国民收入的贡献

我们可以从图1看出，农业在赞比亚国民收入中所占的比重已呈稳定状态（约21%），但它一直以来都对国民收入作出了积极的贡献。值得关注的是，尽管在最近几年赞比亚风调雨顺，农业部门每年的表现却不尽相同。不过在2010年和2011年还是获得了大丰收。

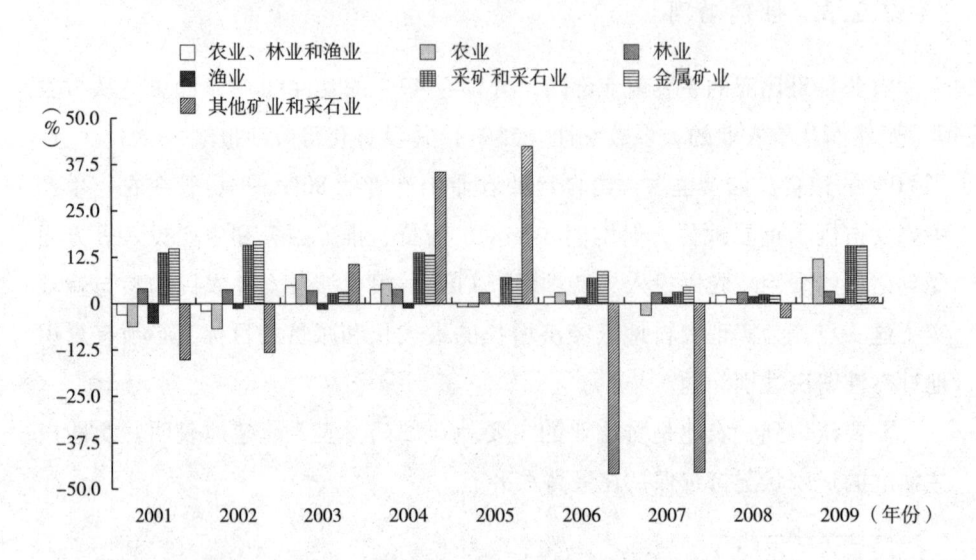

图1　实际GDP中各生产部门的贡献率

资料来源：《赞比亚人类发展报告》，联合国开发计划署，2011。

2.3.2 农业对减贫的贡献

在赞比亚的第六个国家发展计划中,农业已经被视为实现经济可持续增长并最终降低国家贫困水平的一个关键部门。农业部门的持续增长将使农民获得更高的收入,由此改善他们的生计。

尽管农业对国民收入作出了积极的贡献,但赞比亚的贫困水平仍然很高,联合国开发计划署2011年发表的《赞比亚人类发展报告》证实了这一点。报告指出:

- 2006年赞比亚58.3%的人口生活在贫困家庭里,而2004年则是56.3%;
- 2006年穷人平均贫困的指标权重是44%,相比之下,2004年是42.8%;
- 2006年总人口中,多维度贫困指数(根据被剥夺的强度核算)比重[①]是0.257,而2004年是0.241。

居高不下的贫困水平表明赞比亚农业部门的表现不是很好,它未能创造大量就业机会,这一点,在农村地区尤为显著,那里大多数人的收入都来自于农业。这表明,为实现赞比亚经济的合理增长还需要做许多工作。

表4 2006~2011年减贫计划在各部门的资金分配

单位:%,亿克瓦查

类　别	2006年	2007年	2008年	2009年	2010年
对灌溉的支持	0.7	2.4	2	1	0.1
农业的商品化	2.2	2.6	2.2	0	0
动物疾病控制	1.5	1.6	3.3	4.2	2.5
畜牧业发展	0	0.9	0.6	0.6	0.4
化肥支持计划	74	38.2	62.2	75.6	78

[①] 多维度贫困指数(MPI)是衡量个体在健康、教育和生活水平等方面多重被剥夺状况的指标。

续表

类　　别	2006 年	2007 年	2008 年	2009 年	2010 年
战略粮食储备	18.6	52.1	26.9	17.4	18.1
合作教育和培训	0.3	0.7	0.2	0	0
其他	2.2	0.7	2.7	0	0.9
总　　计	100	99.2	100.1	98.8	100
赞币总计	1988	1960	1982	1966	1999

资料来源：农业咨询论坛/食品安全研究项目，2006~2010。

表4说明，2006~2010年，减贫计划（包括对灌溉的支持、土地开发、化肥支持计划等上表中涉及的项目）的拨款保持了持续增长的势头。大部分的拨款流向了化肥支持计划和战略粮食储备。2010年，这两项共占据了扶贫资金的92.1%，其余五项只占7.4%。①

联合国开发计划署2011年发布的《赞比亚人类发展报告》对表4进行了分析，得出的结论是：2006~2010年，减贫资金分配不均的情况有所缓解，政府减少了对灌溉和畜牧支持等服务的资金投入。虽然赞比亚玉米产量有所增加，但可能是以不平等的加剧为代价的，因为定价政策事实上使得收益从玉米消费者向从事大规模生产的商业种植农户转移。联合国开发计划署的报告还表明，提高生产率的关键领域，如农作物科学、推广计划、基础设施建设和稳定而有利的政策环境等领域，没有得到所需的支持。

2.3.3　农业对粮食安全和营养状况的贡献

联合国开发计划署的《赞比亚人类发展报告》清楚地表明，一方面，近期，随着赞比亚农作物产量的提高（大丰收），粮食安全也得到了改善，至少在宏观层面上看是这样的。另一方面，从微观层面上看，粮食安全还取决于

---

① 按照表4数据，肥料支持计划和战略粮食储备两项花销占比应为96.1%，其余五项相加占3.9%。——译者注

其他因素，如从事粮食生产的农户和非粮食作物生产农户的比例、出口倾向性和家庭层面权力的性别分配等。在赞比亚，这些因素交织在一起，共同导致了微观层面的粮食不安全状况成为一个主要问题。①

居民粮食和营养状况的一个指标是粮食贫困人口总数（food poverty headcount）。赞比亚的粮食贫困人口总数不仅高于整体贫困水平，而且在过去几年里下降得很慢。② 这说明即便1996~2006年整体贫困减少了8.8%，但是粮食贫困人口总数只下降了6.3%。③

---

① 《赞比亚人类发展报告》，联合国开发计划署，2011。
② 《赞比亚人类发展报告》，联合国开发计划署，2011。
③ 《赞比亚人类发展报告》，联合国开发计划署，2011。

3 提高小规模生产的政策和制度体系

3.1 政策体系

通过分析现有的政策体系，评估它们是否有助于促进农业在价值链三个阶段（即投入阶段、产出阶段和市场阶段）的发展，尤其要评估小规模的生产者是否会受益于这些措施，是极为重要的。以下是涉及赞比亚农业部门的一些关键性政策。

3.1.1 国家农业政策（2004~2015）

国家农业政策的总体目标是支持和促进一个具有可持续性和竞争力的农业部门的发展，以确保赞比亚的粮食安全。为实现这一目标，应从以下几项具体目标着手：

- 为确保国家和家庭粮食安全，以有竞争力的价格对基本食品的充足供应实行全年度的生产和收获后管理；
- 为推动工业的可持续发展，提供本地生产的农业原材料；
- 增加农产品的出口，提高农业部门对国家收支平衡的贡献率；
- 提高农业产量和生产率以增加收入和就业；
- 确保现有的农业资源基地得到维护和改进。

这些政策影响了农业活动在三个阶段开展的方式。在投入阶段，其中一项规定旨在防治害虫及作物和牲畜的疾病。为实现这一目标，政策规定：在优先发展区域，对于会对经济产生重要影响的疾病，要加强对其疾控和传疾生物控制项目的监督、管理与促进工作。确保农作物和牲畜免受疾病的侵袭十分重要，因为这决定了农业活动能在多大程度上被转化成生产成果。因此，这一政策确定的关键生产投入是农民可以获得农业杀虫剂和兽药。此外，该政策还寻求开发与推广植物和草本制作的兽药的使用。

促进灌溉也是该政策确定的一个关键性举措，这将有助于在投入阶段提高农业发展水平。鉴于赞比亚不时发生严重干旱，可能导致农业产量的下降和牲畜的损失，政策规定政府要充分有效地利用国家丰富的地上和地下水资源，通过发展灌溉来保证全年农业生产。这对小农有着特殊的意义，使得他们能够率先改善家庭的粮食安全和收入状况。

在保证农民可以获得种子方面，该政策也做出了详细的规定。尤其重要的是，政策提出的措施有助于保证农民通过正式和非正式渠道获得种子。政策规定，种子部门将通过种子试验、检验、品种登记、品种保护、执行种子质量标准等措施促进种子贸易、检疫以及其他相关事宜的发展。这些举措至关重要，因为它们有助于保证正式的种子市场继续使用最适合当地环境条件的种子来提高农业产量。

通过直接从研究机构中获得种畜/种子，该政策也促进了非正式种子部门的发展。此外，该政策希望协调种子部门来创造一个可持续发展的农村种子产业。这项举措有着重要的意义，主要是因为许多农民依赖非正式来源种子的使用，其中包括前一收获季节保存下来的未经认证的种子，这些种子没有经过任何测试和品种控制。这一政策下的诸项措施将减少农民对非正式来源的种子的过分依赖。

该政策也承认转基因技术的发展，制定了关于转基因作物种子的繁殖、交易和种子采用等规则。转基因作物虽未被禁止，但受到政府监管，这意味着赞比亚农民在国际市场上仍有保持竞争力的空间。转基因作物的成熟时间缩短，降低了农民的生产成本。这样，农民在国际市场上将会更有竞争力。然而，有人担心转基因作物可能存在健康隐患，这恰好证明了这一政策提出对其进行监管的必要性。

该政策还制定了管理农事活动方面的规定。提高生产效率的一个关键要求是具备专业的知识技能，该政策承认赞比亚大多数农民缺乏利用现有的市场条件、服务并提升自身技能的能力。所以一个有效的推广和信息系统是发展农业不可或缺的要素。这项政策旨在发展和壮大农民组织与农民田间学校以实现技术转移的策略，也包括使用电子和印刷媒介的传播工具，以支持信息的扩展和传递。

该政策也承认政府本身在提供推广服务的能力上存在一定的局限性。因此，该政策还意在促进和鼓励私营部门和非政府组织来参与提供推广服务，虽然对他们的参与尚没有制定相应的协调和监管措施。其他提高产量的举措包括促进作物的多样化种植、使用改良技术以及在小农当中进行技能培训和技术转让，让员工在农民培训机构（Farmer Training Institutes）接受培训，农民则在农民培训中心（Farmer Training Centres）接受培训。

> 对于私营部门和非政府组织参与推广服务，国家发展政策未制定相关措施进行协调和监管

该政策还认识到了畜牧业的重要性，并提供了相关对策来提高牲畜产量。具体包括制作相关的推广性材料/手册，发放给农民和实地工作人员，监控牲畜、牲畜产品和饲料的质量，鼓励私营部门参与提供牲畜养殖和推广服务，促进牲畜和牲畜产品的市场营销。

资金的获取仍是农民面临的严峻挑战之一。该政策制定了相应的策略，帮助农民获取资金。农业政策对农业信贷和金融也做出了规定，包括创建一个基金会，农民通过适当的金融机构和非政府组织可获得资金。此外，该政策采取措施鼓励团体贷款，以保证良好的回报率，并在信贷供应和储蓄动员方面促进私人/公共部门的合作。以上措施若得以实施，将对提高农业产出作出巨大的贡献。

该政策为促进农产品的营销也制定了相应的规定。在产品营销上，政策的目标是促进竞争性的、高效透明的公共和私营部门的发展，让这些部门来驱动农产品和投入的市场化。在这方面，该政策旨在切实落实有关促进各地

区利益相关者之间市场信息流动的策略。此外，该政策还瞄准农村基础设施的建设，如铺设道路、建设农村仓储设施和发展市场中心。为鼓励生产，该政策还致力于建立有保证的农业投入与产出的市场，特别是针对农村地区的小规模农户。其中包括在国内和出口市场上对农作物进行推广。

3.1.2 灌溉政策（2004）

赞比亚灌溉政策的总体目标是建立一个规范的、营利性的灌溉部门，以吸引私人投资者和赞比亚的发展伙伴。然而，这一目标的最终实现却面临大量挑战，且多与小生产者相关。例如，该政策指出，赞比亚法律执行不力，水资源管理和分配不公平，经济效益低，很难吸引小生产者的参与。如果相关政策法律能够得到很好的执行，这些小生产者就能从灌溉农业中获益。

此外，该政策还指出，在农业投资方面仍存在许多挑战，例如发放短期许可证（一般是5年）的行政惯例会阻碍农业投资。如果增加对农业部门的投资，小生产者就能从中获益，因为投资的增加能够扩大对农产品的需求，进而为农民创造更大的市场。所以，小生产者是否受益取决于灌溉政策在多大程度上能解决这些问题。

为实现建立规范化、营利性灌溉部门的总体目标，灌溉政策也设定了一些中期目标，其中包括建立一个程序高效透明的服务性机构，该机构由需求推动建立，农民可以从中获取服务。小生产者面临的主要挑战之一是如何与这些乐于回应其需求的机构建立联系。因此，如果需求驱动型机构能够建立起来，将更好地满足属于赞比亚农民主体的小农的需求。这一政策也确认灌溉产品在赞比亚市场链中能带来附加值，并将其确定为一个目标。影响小农生产力的一个关键问题是市场链不清晰，通过市场链实现农业生产的平稳转变总是存在问题。例如，如果农民在不了解替代市场的情况下就进行耕种，易腐农产品很容易在寻找市场的过程中腐坏变质。通过灌溉政策来解决这种问题，就会对解决小农生产者的困境大有裨益。

基于灌溉政策而制定的举措如成功实施，将有利于提高小农生产者的生活水平。灌溉政策为所有农民制定了综合措施，同时也针对三种不同类别的农民设计了不同的目标和策略。适用于所有农民的综合措施包括重组生产和销售灌溉农产品所需的服务。这一策略的实施将有助于解决农业部门中与农产品销售有关的许多僵化问题和瓶颈问题。另一项重要举措是引入合适的商业信用机制以满足当前及将来灌溉领域私人投资者的需求。鉴于政府财力有限，吸引私人投资十分重要。在这一政策下，通过捋顺市场、提供有增值机会的投资，能够吸引私人投资者。综合策略还包括：放宽政府对投入成本的管制和修改现有水价结构等。这项政策唯一的问题是，它并未制定在灌溉领域吸引私人投资的具体策略，也没有指出这些投资的赢利途径。

在一些从事商业种植农户占大多数的地方，该政策还针对这些新兴农户制定了单独的策略。尽管与传统农民和已经商业化的农民相比，这些新兴农民耕作的土地微不足道，但作为两者之间的过渡，他们的地位依然十分重要。这些新兴农民所面临的问题包括信息匮乏、推广服务支持不足、基础设施落后、融资和组织困难，以及追求暴利的商人造成的剥削性的、不公平的封闭市场等。所以，该政策的核心目标是利用改进后的灌溉技术和服务来扩大新兴农民的生产基地，提高其生产力。为了使新兴农民获益，该政策力图使其获得更多灌溉投入、技术、服务和接受培训的机会，同时获得更加合适的信用机制。所有这些改进，都以强化规范机制为前提，保证从事灌溉农业生产的农民能够公平地获得所需的商品和服务。为实现这些目标，具体做法如下：

● 建立灌溉管理组织以及一个适应性强的法律体制，承认、保护并规范这些组织及其成员，特别是对于女性成员的保护；

● 制定有关用水权的法律，保证所有使用群体公平地获取水资源，避免少数人的特权；

● 确定由国家计划向新兴农民群体转变的可行方式，此后，开放国营农场给新兴农民使用；

● 为农业生产提供生产和加工灌溉作物的信息；

● 使农民能够在收获后及农业加工方面获得更多信息和相关设备；

● 建立并加强监管体制，以保护新兴农民免受中间人的剥削。

灌溉政策也顾及传统农民的利益,传统农民在村舍中从事自给自足的生产,仅将剩余农产品投放到市场中。传统农民主要利用公共基础设施(如小型水渠)从小水坝引水灌溉。然而,许多公共基础设施主要依靠公用事业支出维持,目前已经破旧且无法使用。所以,针对传统农民的灌溉政策的总体目标是使他们能够开发和利用灌溉及其他水资源管理技术,以减轻贫困,保证粮食安全。在灌溉政策下,除了横向交叉的策略以外,有关传统农民的策略还包括:建立相关法律制度,对灌溉管理组织及人员的设立、法律地位、组织结构和授权进行规范;更新与灌溉工程的规划、设计和建设相关的原则和指导方针,加入对受益人意见的征询程序,对其需求做出反应,并使其能够参与其中;修复并升级现有灌溉工程。然而,在这一政策下,只有在用户有强烈需求的情况下,才可能恢复灌溉工程;同时,用户群体对他们预期的参与程度以及在工程建成前后及建设中的责任归属都非常敏感;另外,该恢复工程必须是可行的。这些条件叠加在一起,有可能使政策的实施者非常谨慎,这便导致无法获得所需信息也无法要求恢复工程的传统农民处于更不利的地位。

> 该政策表明,发展灌溉技术和服务确实有利于扩展生产基地和提高新兴农民生产力

因此,和国家农业政策一样,灌溉政策还有非常大的余地惠及小生产者和传统农民。当然,要使该政策能够更有效地实现其宏伟目标,赞比亚仍然需要克服一些严重问题。

3.1.3 国家种子产业政策(1999)

赞比亚国家农业政策指出,农民能够得到种子是十分重要的,这不仅关系到政策目标的实现,也关系到赞比亚的粮食安全。为此,赞比亚制定了国家种子政策,其总体目标是保证农民能够以一种高效便捷的方式获得各种农作物的优质种子,以增加农作物产量,提高农业生产力。为实现这一总体目标,需首先实现一些对小农生产者有利的中期目标。其中包括保证可行、高效、可持续的优质农作物种子生产和供应体系的发展,以满足全国的种子需

求。由于种子短缺会导致种子价格居高不下，迫使农民更多采用传统方式获得种子。而这一举措的实施将有助于赞比亚提高农业产量。

这项政策还旨在建立一个促进正式和非正式体系融合的种子产业。对非正式体制的承认，是保证农民能够获得种子的有效举措，因为利用之前收获的粮食充当种子或从其他农民那里借用种子是农民们常用的非正式渠道。

了解到这些，具体的政策才能通过策略得以实现。例如，政府将继续参与农作物研究，更多地关注传统作物及小规模作物的长期战略性研究，因为这些作物对小农生产者和弱势群体的粮食安全有重要作用，政府也会更多地关注那些私营部门不感兴趣的研究领域。由于小农生产者更乐于选购低成本的种子品种，他们可能会发现私营部门所介绍的种子非常昂贵。所以，政府继续参与农作物研究受到农民的欢迎。

尽管种子产业政策规定政府将继续参与研究，但它也同时规定政府应在不亏本的基础上通过保持品种纯度来支持私人研究的发展。此外，它还规定政府应促进非正式部门的发展，为其提供种畜或基本的种子，否则他们可能无法在不亏本的基础上发展下去。

鉴于大多数农民和种子用户可能缺少相关的科学信息，政府应加强信息的收集和传播工作，从而使最终的使用者和研究者更易获取相关的科学信息和技术。政府的这些举措是非常重要的，因为改良后的种子品种使用率较低，特别是那些小农生产者往往对于这些改良后的种子一无所知。

> 种子产业的成功也离不开私营部门的参与

种子产业的成功也离不开私营部门的参与。利用种子政策为私营部门的参与创造有利的环境是十分重要的。在这方面，政策规定，政府将允许私营部门自由获得不同作物的可用胚质，以鼓励私营部门参与研究。政府还将鼓励私营部门参与应用性研究、农作物改良和品种开发。

该政策还保障农民免受假种子以及未经充分检验的种子的危害。该政策将实现品种发布委员会（Variety Release Committee）制度的正规化，以使利益相关者更多地参与进来。此外，政府还要每年更新种子品种的清单，以保护农民的利益。负责监管种子产业总体发展和运作的国家种子委员会（National Seeds Committee），就有关种子产业的政策问题向政府提出建议，审查种子政策，提高各地区种子产业的实力。

为培养种子产业的创业精神，政府应鼓励成立小型种子企业。而且，政府还应当实行一些监控措施，如建立论坛，来协调非正式体制下的非政府组织，以保障种子企业的正常活动，创建一个可持续发展的乡村种子产业。最重要的是，种子产业的发展和绩效在很大程度上依赖于基础设施的发展水平，所以，在农村地区应发展基础设施特别是道路交通，以鼓励和促进农业发展。

3.1.4 国家合作发展政策（2011）

成立合作社是一项关键性举措，因为通过合作，农业领域的小农生产者能够实现转型。例如，在这一政策下建立的下述类型的服务合作社将有助于提升小农生产者在市场链中的地位。

- 销售与供应合作社（Marketing and Supply Co-operatives）——销售合作社成员所生产的农作物。相比于农民自己销售并听任那些能轻易剥削他们的中间人摆布的情况，这些合作社能增加农民的议价能力，这一点非常重要。

- 运输合作社（Transport Co-operatives）——为运送合作社成员所生产的农作物而对交通工具进行协调管理的合作社。由于基础设施网络落后，农民经常面临如何运输自己所生产的农作物的困境，并不得不因为运输花费大量金钱。利用合作社进行运输可以省下中间商费用，显著降低运输成本。

> 这一政策的总体目标是为自主、透明、可行且需求驱动型的合作社的发展创造一个有利的制度和法制的环境，从而为社会经济发展和减贫作出贡献

- 储蓄与信贷合作社（Savings and Credit Co-operatives）——成员将其储蓄集中起来，彼此贷款。农业需要一定的投资，农民可以利用信贷为农业活动提供资金。许多农民经常无法从事农业生产，很大程度上是因为他们无法负担一些与农业投入相关的花费。因此，这些合作将有助于保证农民获得

成本更低的贷款。

制定措施鼓励成立合作社并规范其运营十分重要。2011年11月，赞比亚农牧业部制定了国家合作发展政策。这一政策的总体目标是：为自主、透明、可行、需求驱动型的合作社的发展创造一个有利的制度和法律环境，从而为发展社会经济和减贫作出贡献。这一总体目标将通过下述中期目标的实现而实现：

- 在国家发展的背景下，创造一个新的体制，改进和重新定位合作化运动；
- 帮助形成一种需求驱动型的、成员领导的、自主的、可行且可持续的合作社；
- 促进合作社活动的多元化；
- 为建立一个有效的合作体系创造有利的环境；
- 为促进合作社的发展提供一个高效的资源调动机制；
- 促进服务提供中的内外联系与合作；
- 除农业合作社外，鼓励建立其他类型的合作社。

为实现上述目标，一项举措是完善相应的法律和制度框架，以促进合作组织的重新定位和改革。这一举措基于这样一种认识，即现有的法律框架不适合促进合作社的发展。此外，该政策希望保证负责合作社的有关部门能在全国各地区实际建立分支部门，并通过实地派驻人员直接处理合作社事项。这将有助于通过监管来加强合作社的运作。

由于在实施中需要参考国际上的最优方法，该政策还规定了发展教育与培训项目，以及提供满足合作社成员需要以及适应当前社会经济环境的数据。与此密切相关的，是促进预备合作社组织的成立，为合作社的成功运营做充分的准备。

如同其他相关农业政策一样，国家合作发展政策也采取一些关键措施来保证农业部门的发展。因此，农牧业部在多大程度上实施这些措施将决定这些政策能否取得成功。

3.2 组织机构

通过评估各机构在农业领域的不同职能，很容易找出在赞比亚农业部门发展中扮演积极角色的关键机构。农牧业部是第 3.1 节中提到的政策的执行机构，但还需要许多其他机构来补充政府工作。其中一项职能是提供农业推广服务。通常是农业与合作部会通过其国家级、省级、地方级网络向农民提供推广服务和信息数据，农民组织、私营部门、非政府组织和社区组织也会帮助农民获得推广服务。

农业部门的另外一项重要职能是向农民提供优质种子。在这方面对农牧业部起到辅助和补充作用的机构包括：种子管理与认证协会（SCCI），它负责种子质量管理、监控种子贸易以及部门协调；国家植物基因资源中心（National Plant Genetic Resource Centre），负责采集和保存基因资源；其他研究机构负责品种的开发与改良。私营种子公司、非政府组织、社区组织也积极参与，它们主要负责种子的生产、营销和分配。

保证农民有适宜的土壤耕作也是农业部门的一项重要职责。在此方面发挥作用的机构有农牧业部下设的土壤与农作物研究司（Soil and Crops Research Branch of the MAL），该司对各农业生态区土壤和作物进行比较优势研究。赞比亚其他重要的农作物研究机构还有研究基金（Research Trusts）、赞比亚大学（University of Zambia）、国家科学技术委员会（NSTC）科技与职业培训部、国家科学与工业研究院（NISIR），以及一些种子公司。

灌溉的发展由归属农牧业部的技术服务司（TSB）主导，能源与水利开发部和赞比亚环境管理署（ZEMA）亦参与其中。土地耕种的管理与开发方面存在着相同的模式：主要由技术服务司负责提供土地耕种服务，土地部（Ministry of Lands），工程与供应部（Ministry of Works and Supply），旅游、环境与自然资源部（Ministry of Tourism, Environment and Natural Resources），以及赞比亚环境管理局协同工作。

农业培训也是确保生产力提高的最重要职能之一。赞比亚有多个机构提供农业教育培训，包括赞比亚大学（学位层次）、自然资源开发学院（文凭层次)、姆皮卡与蒙泽农业学院(证书层次)。赞比亚大学(学位层次)和赞比亚动物卫生研究所(证书层次)提供兽医培训。其他相关机构还包括卡卢卢希(Kalulushi)、查普拉(Chapula)与卡萨卡(Kasaka)农场培训学院,帕拉巴纳畜牧业发展信托基金和农业培训中心(Chapula and Kasaka Farm Training Institutes),它们还提供短期的、根据需求设定的课程。合作社教育培训由合作社学院、卡泰特营销与合作社中心(Katete Centre of Marketing)以及卡布兰旺达合作社培训中心(Kabulamwanda Co-operative Training Centre)提供。

总体而言,这些机构在实现各种农业政策所制定的农业发展目标中起了关键作用。所以,在实现这些目标的过程中,这些机构提供教育培训的能力对于实现目标也是非常重要的。

3.3 实施策略

在实现上述目标过程中,农牧业部(Ministry of Agriculture and Livestock)开展了多项活动和项目。这些项目中,以下项目得到了很多支持。

农民投入支持项目(FISP)

众所周知,信贷在赞比亚供不应求,即使能申请到,利息也是非常高昂的。2002年以来,赞比亚政府一直试图通过农牧业部向农民提供信贷来填补无法获得信贷的空白。[①] 通过农民投入支持项目,政府一直向许多处于弱势却能自力更生的小农提供化肥和改良种子。

该项目旨在提高农业劳动生产率、农民收入、粮食安全并帮助开发投入市场。到目前为止,这种补贴已经产生积极的效果,尤其增加了赞比亚的玉米产量。但它对农业生产率和减贫的影响很小。[②] 此外,农业咨询论坛的调查结果表明,当前实施此项目的方式还存在很多问题,如国库成本高,投资意

[①] J. 法林顿、O. 萨萨:《赞比亚农业改革的驱动力:辨析塑造政策环境的因素》,英国国际发展署,2002。

[②] 尼古拉斯·J. 席塔克等:《在赞比亚通过电子凭证制度实施"农民投入支持项目"的可行性评估》,印达巴农业政策研究所第53期政策简报,2012年4月。

向目标不明确，实际投入延迟，投资利用率差，排挤私营部门，对推广部门的官员要求严苛，并且阻碍农业的多样化。

粮食储备署（FRA）

赞比亚政府在多党民主运动执政时期建立了赞比亚国家粮食储备署（FRA），其唯一目的是保证国内有足够的玉米来保障粮食安全。

该机构的成立是为保障国家的粮食安全，而非管理玉米市场。萨萨、法林顿2002年合著的《赞比亚农业改革的驱动力：辨析塑造政策环境的因素》报告指出，这一机构的主要职能是在国家无法得到充足的玉米时予以补救，那时新出现的私营部门也无力充分满足市场对玉米的需求。[①] 不可否认，该机构当初成立的唯一目的是粮食储备，但现在，它已经成为一个市场管理的工具。粮食储备署参与市场交易的弊端已经得到了认识：它排挤预期的投资，而这些投资对小农生产者扩大市场机遇、提供体制所需的高效的前后联系都是必要的。

批评人士指出，国家粮食储备署的存在阻碍了私营贸易的发展，导致磨坊主、农民、中间人或能够接触到国内外市场的农民彼此间不能够进行互动。类似的批评之声早在2000年就已经出现。2002年，萨萨、法林顿在报告中称，"如果私营部门能在一个自由市场经济中独立运营，而政府只提供规范的监管，那么私营部门就会有发展的动力，并可能有发展的能力"。[②]

粮食安全一揽子项目

作为农牧业部项目的补充，社区发展与社会服务部（Ministry of Community Development and Social Services）于2000年创立了该项目，意在增强两类农民的能力，一类是脆弱却仍能自力更生的农民，他们因恶劣的天气条件而失

[①] J. 法林顿、O. 萨萨：《赞比亚农业改革的驱动力：辨析塑造政策环境的因素》，英国国际发展署，2002。

[②] J. 法林顿、O. 萨萨：《赞比亚农业改革的驱动力：辨析塑造政策环境的因素》，英国国际发展署，2002。

去生产资源；一类是那些受到结构调整改革所带来的负面影响的农民，他们获得的投入和服务因之而减少。

最初，这个项目是一项生计发展战略，意在使农民从自给自足生产转变为剩余产品生产；而现在，毫无疑问，这一项目已经成为赞比亚社会安全网络的核心部分。在此项目下，政府向贫困家庭提供种子和化肥等生产性投入，其主要目标是通过提高生产率和家庭粮食安全使目标家庭实现自立自足。

此外，《赞比亚农业改革的驱动力：辨析塑造政策环境的因素》也认为，该项目现在是一项社会安全网项目，其主旨是通过向弱势家庭提供经济增长和减贫手段来达到提高他们生产力和实现家庭粮食安全的目的。[①]

[①] J. 法林顿、O. 萨萨：《赞比亚农业改革的驱动力：辨析塑造政策环境的因素》，英国国际发展署，2002。

4

农业投资

根据经济合作与发展组织（OECD）2012年发表的《赞比亚投资政策评估》，投资政策的全面性直接影响到投资水平，包括当地投资和外国投资。透明性、产权保护和非歧视原则是建立良好的投资环境所需的关键性投资政策原则。

正如国家农业政策指出的，农牧业部会游说财政与国家规划部（Ministry of Finance and National Planning）和其他利益相关方，通过预算拨款激励农业投资，例如税收优惠和农业进出口激励措施。农业部门也将扮演营销机构的角色，帮助潜在的农业投资者与赞比亚投资中心建立联系，并帮助传播有关投资机会和激励措施方面的信息。

农业商业化计划（ACP）和国家农业合作政策（2004）号召发展高效的、竞争性的、可持续的农业，二者都将发展高潜力农业地区的基础设施、加强农业合作社及农民组织的建设视为达成这一目标的重要举措。[1]

赞比亚政府在给农业投资创造必要的环境方面已经取得了很大进展。一个例子就是2002年出台的"农业区块"（Farm Block）提案，旨在将农业用地商业化、开拓农村地区以及吸引投资。[2] 根据赞比亚发展署的网站报道，8块农业区的商业开发已经启动，为流向私营部门的大规模投资提供土地。整

---

[1] 《赞比亚投资政策评估》，经济合作与发展组织，2012。
[2] 《贫瘠土地治理系统下的大规模农业投资：赞比亚案例中的参与者与组织机构》，世界银行土地与贫困年度会议论文，华盛顿：世界银行，2012年4月23~26日。

个农业区块预计约10万公顷，私人投资者将通过适当的基础设施建设来实现农场的商业化，而基础设施建设也将有利于这些私营投资者的农业经营活动。农业区块的商业化将有助于小、中、大型生产规模的农民通过种植计划从事针对国内外市场的商品化的农业活动。这也使得政府通过进行基础设施建设将公有土地转化成国有土地。

根据2012年赞比亚投资指南，赞比亚政府已经出台了多项激励措施来鼓励农业领域投资，这些措施如下。

- 在农业生产经营之前，保证免征4年投入税。
- 农产品和农用物资出口零税率。
- 一些农业设备和农用机械的进口增值税可以延期征收。
- 所得税税率为10%。
- 对修建栏杆、砖或石墙给予100%的改善农场津贴，给获得农场的农场工人1000万克瓦查的津贴。
- 为农场改造提供100%的津贴，如清除树桩、防治水土流失工程、钻孔打井、航空和地球物理调查、水资源保护等工作。
- 在分销公司开始经营农场的前5年，农场收益的红利将免税。
- 任何种植茶叶、咖啡、香蕉、柑橘或类似作物的人可以得到发展津贴，此类津贴的10%将被用于调查该产业的收益和利润。
- 灌溉设备进口免税，其他农业设备的进口税率也有降低。
- 预混合料、动物饲料的维生素添加剂关税减免5%。

尽管存在这些激励措施，小农生产者依然无法跟上能够帮助提高生产率的科技发展的步伐。不言而喻，小农生产者只能依靠传统农业生产方式，在自己的农场上生产出足够的粮食作物来满足自己的消费。

2011/2012年度的粮食预期调查显示，大部分小农种植的作物，如玉米、小米和棉花等，与那些被商业化农民高度垄断经营的大豆和小麦相比，都只有很低的利润收入。100%的小麦产出和93%的大豆产出都产自商业化农民，这些作物拥有相对较好的价格和市场。显然，因为缺少浇灌技术的实力，赞比亚的小农们是无力生产冬小麦的（冬小麦的成败端赖浇灌）。至于大豆，作为一种非传统的作物，人们需要对其种植的方式有更深入的了解，同时也需要探索可能的市场。

2011/2012年度的农作物预测调查表明，小农生产者正面临着生产力水平低下的困境。根据齐沙拉（Chishala）在《赞比亚农业技术传播状况分析》中的分析，"如果小农生产者能获得充足的信息和资源来高效地生产运作，那么他们的农业生产力可以得到提高"。[1] 影响生产力的一个明显因素在于政府研究机构没有充足的资金支持科技研发，科技发展水平低对小农生产者产生了消极影响。这意味着该领域迫切需要投资。

在赞比亚，投资者有几种不同的方法可以获得土地，这取决于土地是国有土地还是社区的公有土地。[2] 对于国有土地而言，投资者可以联系赞比亚发展署，该机构会指导投资者哪些土地可以投资。此外，潜在投资者也可以找到国有土地现在的所有者，并就土地转让进行商业谈判。投资者也可以直接接触村长和酋长来最终获得社区公有土地。但是，社区公有土地在转让前需转化为国有土地，而这个过程未必能符合"负责任农业投资原则"。

关于齐杨西灌溉工程案例的研究也可以被用来评估赞比亚投资的性质，这一灌溉工程位于赞比亚卡富埃地区，毗邻卡富埃河。2012年，消费者团结与信托协会主持了一项研究计划，其中包括对受益农民的深度访谈。考察结果用于评估该工程是否严格遵循了"负责任农业投资原则"。这一工程由非洲基础设施有限公司（InfraCo）[3] 主持，预计投入2900万美元，其中荷兰政府将投入1050万美元。

这一工程已经取得了一些效益，效益甚至可以超过该投资造成的负面问题。合作社现在持有非洲农业有限公司（FarmCo）25%的股权，而给当地人的股息已稳定在25万克瓦查左右。本章节的目的在于评估投资计划在何种程

---

[1] 齐沙拉：《赞比亚农业技术传播状况分析》，南非发展共同体，2007。
[2] 《贫瘠土地治理系统下的大规模农业投资：赞比亚案例中的参与者与组织机构》，世界银行土地与贫困年度会议论文，华盛顿：世界银行，2012年4月23～26日。
[3] "InfraCo Africa"是由荷兰、瑞士、瑞典、世界银行等捐助者合资成立的关注非洲基础设施发展的有限公司。——译者注

度上符合"负责任农业投资原则"。

正如前面所提到的,"负责任农业投资原则"包括七条,农业投资遵守了第五、六条原则,而下述原则存在一些灰色区域,需要进一步完善。

- 原则一:承认和尊重现存的对土地及其相关自然资源的权利。

承认此项原则的投资必须确认所有的土地所有人,还必须在当事者充分知情和自由选择的基础上与土地所有人或使用者进行协商,以确定所要转让的土地权利的类型和形式。

投资者获得社区公有土地的过程常常存在弊端。投资者致信地方议会前,需要向酋长或首领核实这块土地能否转让,以及是否有人认领;在勘测和使用土地前,地方议会需要核实土地的所有权是否存在矛盾之处。但事实上,在投资者到来时,当地通常宣称大多数土地可供转让,酋长往往会首先压制一些不同的声音,特别是只有酋长和投资者在谈判价格。

在建设齐杨西灌溉系统之前,有21户人家占据了大部分的肥沃土地,这些土地被用于多种农业活动,包括农作物生产、牲畜养殖及制造修建房屋所需的砖料。尽管其中20户被重新安置在齐杨西区内,并成为畅杨亚合作社(Chanyanya Cooperative)的成员,但仍有1户拒绝加入。拒绝的原因包括项目产出以及商业农场的红利如何在农民中进行分配尚不明晰。在这项调查进行时,在合作社的125个成员中,只有不到10个小农生产者占有并充分使用20%的土地。这表明,购买土地时,信息并不是对农民完全公开,所以现有的土地权利并未被完全尊重。

同时,调查表明,大约有126人永久性地迁移出自己的家园,他们的土地被捐给了这项工程。这项工程的建造意味着原住民的住所、畜牧用地、农用地遭到破坏,一些家庭被迫失去土地。重新安置他们的土地面积要小于其原有的土地,造成了一些邻里纠纷,特别是牲畜养殖者之间的纠纷,因为牲畜没有足够的活动空间,一些牲畜闯入周围其他人的土地。

- 原则二:投资不会危及粮食安全而会加强粮食安全。

部分畅杨亚合作社的成员已经后悔同意齐杨西投资项目。这项投资使得部分原住民不能再大量种植玉米,因为相比于他们因工程失去的土地,重新安置他们的土地面积较小，而且不够肥沃。一些受访者称，正是这点招致了投资者对他们原有土地的觊觎。一位居民非常恼怒地抱怨说，幸亏项目引进时孩子已经不再在校上学，否则她将没办法支持孩子继续读书，因为她从原来拥有的大块土地上能够获得更多的收入。

尽管曾多次召开会议商讨安置形式，一些相关家庭同意了重新安置的程序，但人们仍认为原住地要比新安置地更加肥沃——这妨碍了部分农户的生产，因为他们无法再像过去一样种植玉米糊口并挣钱。

除了齐杨西项目之外，赞比亚的小农也普遍无法感受到农业部门大规模投资所带来的好处。他们的生产效率没有发生变化，但是他们会抱怨由于商业农场的大规模生产，农产品的价格变低了。这危及了农产品净卖方的生计。①

• 原则三：在一个适合的商业、法律和监管环境下，农业投资相关的过程是透明的、受监控的，并确保涉及所有利益相关者的问责制度。

人们普遍感到齐杨西项目缺少透明度，因为非洲基础设施有限公司提供的关于畅杨亚试点项目中土地数量的资料缺乏一致性。在非洲基础设施有限公司2010年3月出具的齐杨西灌溉工程简报、非洲基础设施有限公司的官方项目网站和非洲基础设施有限公司关于畅杨亚工程的文件中，关于此工程土地分配详情的信息并不一致。

• 原则四：与所有受到重大影响者进行协商，商议达成的协议得到记录和执行。

需要明确的是：第一，程序的要求；第二，此类咨询所达成的协议的特点；第三，协议如何执行。由于土地分属于不同的家庭，这些家庭很难与投资者达成条款和条件相同的协议。一些已完工项目还存在异议，这表明投资实现之前，没有与所有受到影响的人达成协议，所以该项原则没有得到充分的遵守。

• 原则五：投资者要确保项目尊重法治，反映行业的最佳实践，富有高

---

① 阿斯兰·阿斯里汉等：《应对农业土地争夺》，《基尔政策简报》第31期，2011年6月。

度的经济活力，同时能产生持久的共享价值。

- 原则六：投资能产生良好的社会和再分配影响，同时不增加脆弱性。
- 原则七：项目对环境的影响需要被量化，采取措施鼓励资源的可持续利用，同时尽量减少并缓和负面影响。

人们普遍担忧，有关环境的规章条例经常被规避。在赞比亚，大型投资者必须向赞比亚环境管理署（ZEMA）提交一份环境影响评估，但这一规定通常并未执行。尽管存在监管，许多投资者仍在不与赞比亚环境管理署接触的情况下便开始生产。①

---

① 阿斯兰·阿斯里汉等：《应对农业土地争夺》，《基尔政策简报》第31期，2011年6月。

5

实地调查发现

为了了解农民面临的问题,在抽样调查中对 120 名农民进行了访谈,以收集他们的意见和经验。在这 120 名农民中,40 人来自铜带省,40 人来自东部省,40 人来自南部省。此外,对其他的利益相关方也进行了访谈,其中包括地方农业协调办公室、农业咨询论坛、畜牧业发展信托基金、地方农业政策研究所、赞比亚全国农民协会、赞比亚肉牛协会、赞比亚发展署和赞比亚棉花协会。

5.1 投入

5.1.1 土地

采访中对农民的调查结果表明,在赞比亚的农村,小农生产者依靠传统土地所有权制度获得农用土地。在大多数情况下,通常由群体、家族或宗族、家庭或个人持有土地。在当地领导人知情的情况下,社区或村中的个人可以给他人一块土地使用。一旦获得土地,可以一代又一代地使用下去。在这方面,访谈中还向农民询问了其土地所有权的来源(参见图 2)。

在赞比亚,特别是在铜带省、东部省和南部省,土地所有权的主要形式是社区的传统土地所有权。我们的调查结果显示,62.5% 的受访者表示,他们拥有社区的传统土地所有权,而 37.5% 的受访者表示,他们有土地所有权契据。然而,在正式确定土地所有权方面,相比其他两个省份,铜带省已取得了很大进展;总体来看,大约 70% 表示拥有土地所有权契据的农民来自铜

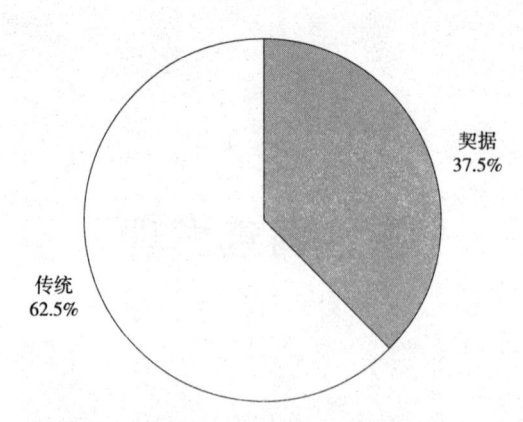

图 2　受采访农民的土地所有权形式分布
资料来源：采访数据。

带省，这并不令人惊讶，因为它是一个以城市为主的省，那里的有些农民之前是矿工，在采矿活动发展迟滞时为了生计转作农民，而且大多数都是被裁矿工。

5.1.2　灌溉

在任何一个国家的农业部门，改进灌溉系统都是促进农业生产的主要驱动力之一。不可否认，赞比亚虽然拥有丰富的水资源，但灌溉部门一直处于停滞状态。开发地下水对于大多数小农生产者来说仍然无法实现。具体来说，在铜带省、南部省和东部省，种植棉花、花生和玉米的小农生产者依赖降雨能取得好收成。当问及农民是否可以实现灌溉时，调查结果表明，那些农民用水桶/水壶进行灌溉（参见图3）。

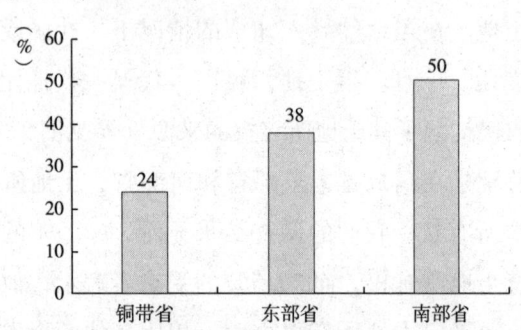

图 3　利用水桶/水壶灌溉的统计
资料来源：采访数据。

调查结果表明，在铜带省、东部省和南部省，分别有24%、38%和50%农民用水桶/水壶灌溉，这意味着，在铜带省、东部省和南部省分别有76%、62%和50%的农民没有进行任何方式的灌溉。在南部省只有1%的小农生产者使用脚踏泵灌溉他们的田地。他们只用这种方法灌溉园艺作物，而没有使用任何方式来灌溉棉花、花生和玉米作物。这也与其他研究得出的结论相符，赞比亚拥有42.3万公顷的水浇地，却只有0.9%的耕地得到灌溉。[①] 这表明，需要采取措施，鼓励对田地和商品作物灌溉的投资。

5.1.3 获得推广服务/投入

通过农牧业部的推广人员向农民提供推广服务是政府的一项重要职责。政府能否有效提供这一重要服务，取决于受过训练的推广人员以及推广服务覆盖的农民数量。在东部省、南部省和铜带省，1名推广人员平均负责1000名农民。农民表示，推广人员一年内平均只来访3次。在铜带省、东部省和南部省，分别有71%、78%和84%的受访农民表示，他们能够享受到推广服务（参见表5）。研究结果表明，距离因素影响到推广服务的提供和获取。这也得到了地方农业协调员的证实，他表示，他们非常缺乏推广人员。

所有接受采访的农民都提到，他们对于获得的推广服务的水平并不满意。

表5 享受推广服务的农户分布

地区（省）	调查户数	享受推广服务的比例（%）	不同距离享受推广服务的比例（%）	
			距离≤5km	距离>5km
铜带省	40	71	100	74
东部省	40	78	100	76
南部省	40	84	100	80

资料来源：采访数据。

[①]《粮价飞涨下的赞比亚国家行动计划》，联合国粮食及农业组织，2009年5月。

图 4 表明，距离对于能否获得推广服务有一定的影响，距离越远，农户获得推广服务的可能性就越小。从南部省的情况看，在 0～5 千米的范围内，能够获得推广服务的农民比例为 100%，在 5～10 千米范围内，其比例降至 85%，超过 10 千米，则降到 75%。从图 4 中还可以看出，这种下降也表现在其他省份。

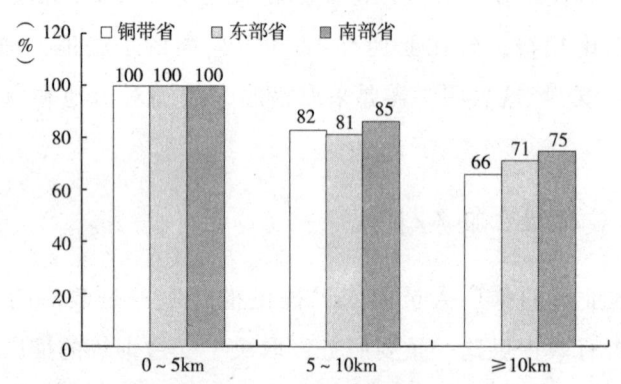

图 4　不同距离的住户可以获得推广服务的百分比
资料来源：采访数据。

投入方面，在对粮食作物的分析中，我们选取了棉花、花生、玉米，在对牲畜的分析中，我们选取了肉牛和山羊。

先从牲畜入手，在山羊的养殖方面，所有的农民都表示他们让山羊自己觅食。在肉牛的饲养方面，在旱季通常采用玉米秸秆喂养和放牧相结合的方式。在雨季，牧场就能够满足牛的需要。因此，几乎所有接受采访的农民对养殖牲畜都没有进行任何投入，严重依赖自然条件。

在棉花种植方面，调查结果表明，所有接受采访的农民都接受轧棉公司的全种植计划的投入。农牧业部表示，棉花行业的特点是轧棉厂家提供有效的投入和推广服务。这些轧棉厂以信贷的形式在正确的时间为农民提供适量的投入。他们还提供推广和销售服务。

接受采访的花生种植户表示，他们使用回收的种子，而且极不愿意采用新改良的品种。在玉米种植中，98% 接受采访的农民表示，他们收到了来自农民投入支持项目的支持，但其中 70% 的农民表示，他们收到的这部分投入不敷所需，因此，他们从农业经销商那里购买化肥和除草剂，以此来补充其得到的补贴性投入。

5.1.4 获得贷款

在赞比亚，正如大多数发展中国家，农民普遍缺乏能够立刻获得现金的渠道以满足自己的需求，主要是农业上的投入需求。因为小农生产者缺乏足够的抵押担保，获得金融机构的贷款困难而又复杂。人们普遍认为，农民难以获得贷款，获得贷款常常要付出高昂的代价。赞比亚政府力图填补农民无法获得贷款的空白，给农民提供补贴性投入。部分小农生产者会得到私人公司的贷款，用以种植棉花等经济作物。

所有接受采访的农民都表示，他们缺乏获得金融机构提供的贷款计划的机会，这是因为在赞比亚的借贷成本高，而且不利于小农。

2008年联合国粮农组织的报告的内容补充了我们的研究，指出赞比亚几乎不存在为小农的牲畜养殖提供的贷款。在农村地区，金融服务的提供一直存在缺口。这是在20世纪90年代中期大多数政府补助的和公有资金的农村金融机构倒闭之后出现的现象。

难以或根本无法获得金融服务阻碍了小农改善、扩大农业生产，实现生产的多样化，以获取足够的收入，改善他们的生活。存在的问题仍然是如何为缺乏抵押资产的小农获得贷款找到解决办法。最近几年已经推出了许多制度革新来解决这个问题，但收效都不太好。

5.1.5 获得兽医服务

赞比亚的兽医服务仍然存在很多不足之处。兽医服务往往被视为政府为发展农业，特别是促进牲畜主要产区的农业发展而采取的政策。[1] 在这方面，农民也被问及能否获得兽医服务的问题（参见表6）。

---

[1] T. 凯琳达等：《土地利用综合评估数据在赞比亚农林政策评估与分析中的运用》，联合国粮食及农业组织，2008。

表6 获得兽医服务的农户分布以及距离与获得兽医服务的关系

地区（省份）	调查户数	获得兽医服务的百分比（%）	不同距离获得兽医服务的百分比（%）	
			距离≤5km	距离>5km
铜带省	40	67	100	63
东部省	40	78	100	75
南部省	40	82	100	81

资料来源：采访数据。

研究结果表明，铜带省与东部省和南部省相比，获得兽医服务的比例是相当低的，三省的比例分别为67%、78%和82%。我们还发现，农民能否获得药物，取决于他们是否有能力购买药物，并要求地方兽医官办公室协助使用这些药物。然而，部分农民已经受过一些使用这些药物的培训。通常在紧急情况下政府才提供服务，例如某种疾病爆发的时候，如科立多病，[①] 手足口病等。在这些省份，人工授精、在杀虫液池中浸洗牲畜都没有得到很好的发展，即使的确有杀虫液池，条件也很恶劣。

统计数据表明，兽医服务资源的分配一直都不能满足需求，这是制约改进和提高农业生产、减少贫困的主要因素之一。在过去3年，只有约6%的财政预算用于农业，因而限制了为家畜疾病控制计划划拨的资金。削减政府开支对于政府在诸如推广服务等农业服务方面的质量和覆盖面有直接影响。如果分析2013年的预算分配，这种情况可能恶化，农业所占的比例由原来的约6.3%降至5.7%。

这反过来对整个农业部门的生产力产生了负面影响。另外，在经济自由化之前，兽医服务等延伸活动能够有效运作。在大多数农村地区，由于缺乏资金，这些服务几乎都已经完全终止。因此，许多养牛的农民已经因为科立多病和其他牲畜疾病损失了很多牛。在南方省等类似的地方，牛群的惨重损失严重影响到经济作物和粮食作物的生产，从而对农民的生计产生了负面影

---

① Corridor Disease 的音译，一种蜱传性原虫病，与非洲罗得西亚热相似，病原为劳氏泰累尔梨浆虫（Theileria Lawrencei）。

响。此外，养殖者、经销商和加工者得到的信贷支持也很有限。①

图 5 所示的调查结果表明，距离对兽医服务的获得有所影响。图 5 表明，距离越远，获得兽医推广服务的小农比例越小。在铜带省，农民得到兽医推广服务的百分比随距离的增加而下降，由 5 千米以内的 100% 下降到 5~10 千米以内的 80%，再降至 10 千米以上的 66%，图中可以看到，其他省份的情况也是如此。

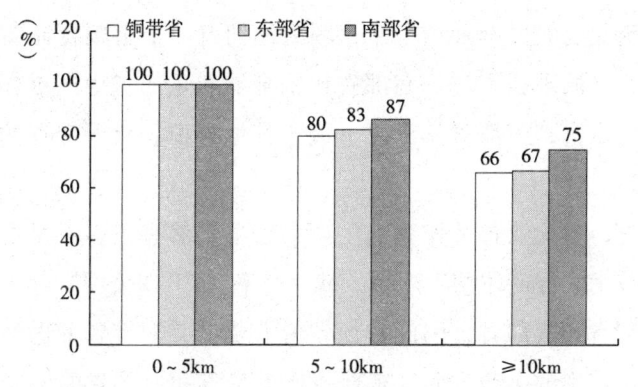

图 5　获得兽医服务的农户百分比与距离的关系
资料来源：采访数据。

5.1.6　能否使用到最就近的永久道路

在赞比亚，农村地区的大多数农民都因其住地的地形以及缺乏耐久的、维护良好的道路，而面临寻找市场的困难。无须赘言，农户需要社会和基础设施方面的支持，才能有效地提高生活水平。此外，社会和基础设施方面的支持包括：投入和产出市场，医疗中心和学校，以及参与政府和非政府组织的支持计划。② 采访中得知，大多数农村地区的道路通常是季节性的砂石路面，也很少得到维护，缺乏耐久的运输设施。不过，在农村地区偶尔可以见

---

① T. 凯琳达等：《土地利用综合评估数据在赞比亚农林政策评估与分析中的运用》，联合国粮食及农业组织，2008。
② T. 凯琳达等：《土地利用综合评估数据在赞比亚农林政策评估与分析中的运用》，联合国粮食及农业组织，2008。

到流动商贩在村子里购买农民的谷物。

所有接受采访的农民都提到,他们有可供使用的道路,但对道路的状况表示担心,这些道路破败不堪。结果是运输成本的增加,导致生产和销售成本的增加。

5.2 产出端

大多数赞比亚农民都种植玉米,因为他们有一个由粮食储备署提供的具有较优市场价格的现成市场。南部省比铜带省和东部省生产更多的玉米。对所预期的销售而言,东部省相比之下逊于其他省份。而铜带省的生产效率比其他省份要高。

总体而言,赞比亚各种作物的生产力水平仍然有很多不足之处。有必要结合适当的技术来提高作物生产率。就生产率(产量/公顷)而言,铜带省的表现优于东部省和南省,因此其他省份需要借鉴铜带省的做法以提高生产率。在棉花和花生的生产方面,东部省比铜带省和南部省的生产率高(参见表7)。

表7 2011/2012 年农作物预测调查

作物	省 份	种植面积(公顷)	收获面积(公顷)	预期产量(吨)	收成(吨/公顷)	预期销售(吨)
玉米	铜带省	89501	79329	205542	2.30	122306
	东部省	276288	245319	572760	2.07	214265
	南部省	303429	227076	554275	1.83	257126
花生	铜带省	8709	8447	5399	0.62	2892
	东部省	56903	54793	30895	0.54	10223
	南部省	22874	20420	9514	0.42	2.040
棉花	铜带省	605	605	785	1.30	—
	东部省	190607	184472	160956	0.84	—
	南部省	40380	36460	33417	0.83	—

资料来源:《农作物预测调查2011/2012》,赞比亚农牧业部,2012。

据赞比亚中央统计办公室的资料，截至 2010 年，全国牛的数量为 303.8 万头，山羊的数量为 758501 只。不可否认，从产值方面看，猪排名第一，山羊排名第二。有必要从商业化方面来看待山羊的养殖，因为通过卡萨姆巴拉萨（Kasumbalesa）和纳孔德（Nakonde）的边境，这类产品有一个巨大的、专业化的出口市场。现有文献表明，畜产品如山羊肉的需求不断增加，可以增加小规模农户参与市场的机会。然而，文献也强调指出，现有的山羊市场在很大程度上是非正式的，投入和服务都十分匮乏。

在三个省份（铜带省、东部省及南部省）的存储设施方面，调查结果显示，农民所使用的存储设备没有得到很好的发展，这也导致农民在收获后损失的增加。有传统存储设施的农民表示，他们在害虫防治、堆垛、记录保存和消防安全方面存在困难，最主要的还是存储空间有限。

畜牧业方面，小规模农户没有冷藏设施。这给小规模农户持续生产山羊肉和牛肉带来困难。

5.3 营销问题

从玉米市场来看，最大市场参与者是通过粮食储备署行事的政府，所有农民都表示，他们对粮食储备署的运作感到不满意，因为该机构没有及时购买他们的产品并及时支付，妨碍他们有效地规划下一季的生产。赞比亚政府通过农牧业部确定玉米的最低价，现在是每 50 千克玉米 6.5 万克瓦查。玉米种植已经吸引了很多农民，因为现成的市场可以提供更好的价格，此外它是赞比亚一项主要的农作物。虽然这个价格很有吸引力，但所有的农民都表示，由于粮食储备署没有及时采购和付款，他们只好接受皮包商提供的 4 万克瓦查的价格，尽管这个价格比粮食储备署的最低价低得多。

但这也有积极的一面。由于政府在玉米行业创造的有利环境，它吸引了大多数小农生产者，所有接受采访的农民都从事玉米的种植，即便他们还可以从事其他的农业活动。这种对玉米种植有利的营销环境排挤了在其他作物上的投资，透过连续下滑的多样化指数也可以看得出来（参见表 8）。

表 8 作物多样化指数

单位：公顷

	2005/2006 年	2006/2007 年	2007/2008 年	2008/2009 年	2009/2010 年	2010/2011 年
其他主要作物	949037	943355	902493	1119465	1133808	1093090
玉米	784524	872812	928224	1125466	1242271	1355764
多样化指数	1.21	1.08	0.97	0.99	0.91	0.81

资料来源：农业咨询论坛，2012。

多样化指数是由某一地区其他作物种植面积除以玉米种植面积而得出的。表8数据显示出玉米种植的增加。

棉花行业由私营部门控制。所有接受采访的农民都表示，他们加入种植计划，并将其产品出售给预先资助他们的轧棉厂。轧棉厂（杜纳万特、嘉吉和联盟三家）是这一领域的主要参与者，它们与农民签订棉花的种植计划协议。根据种植计划，农民在投入端接受贷款和推广服务。通常在设定市场价格时考虑贷款。棉花的市场价格取决于国际市场，只要国际市场上棉花价格下降，农民就会被告知，但是当价格上涨时，这些企业就不愿告知农民国际市场上的有利形势，由此以牺牲小规模农户的利益为代价得到超常利润。缺乏行业透明度导致大多数农民停止生产棉花。

花生行业的营销渠道没有得到很好的发展，这个市场很不正规。农民种植花生，并将其出售给种植其他作物的农民，导致花生以更高的价格在市场上销售。这种作物的市场是现成的。

我们的研究结果表明，主要是妇女在负责播种、除草和收获花生。在销售方面，主要是妇女在城乡市场上从事小规模非正规的花生交易。此外，在铜带省、东部省和南部省，75%的女性户主家庭从事花生的生产和销售。

这一行业的问题是，这些农民无法根据花生的品种和档次对其进行分类，如果他们有这方面的能力，将能最大限度地增加他们的收入。这些农民在收获后对花生的处理方式也存在问题，由此导致了花生黄曲霉素含量的提高，使其达不到国际标准。因此，有必要通过技术投入来处理黄曲霉素，减少花生霉变概率，例如用塑料膜覆盖花生或改进包装。①

农民表示，牛肉具有良好的市场销路，虽然95%的人表示他们继承和饲养牛是出于社会声望的考虑，只在非常需要的时候才会卖掉牛。应采取措施使这一行业的农民知晓养牛商品化的重要性。饲养山羊的农民也一样，他们养羊是为了家庭活动的需要，只在非常需要时才出售山羊。

---

① 尼古拉斯·J. 席塔克等：《技术纲要：对赞比亚农业的描述性统计与分析——基于美国国际开发署代表团"保障未来粮食供给战略评估"》，食品安全研究项目52号工作文件，2011年4月。

6

总结与建议

　　此项研究表明，赞比亚农业部门仍有很大的提升空间，特别是应当更多地关注小农生产者。小农约占农民的70%，主导了玉米、谷子、小米、花生和棉花的种植。本研究确认了一些需要迫切解决的问题，以保证提高小农生产力。例如，灌溉条件差，这可以从小农们使用水桶和水壶进行灌溉得到证明。如果农民使用其他的灌溉措施，如安装水泵、收集并存储雨水，便可以提高生产力。

　　国家农业政策规定将通过种子实验、种子作物检验、品种登记、品种保护和施行种子质量标准等举措，对种子行业进行规范，以促进种子的贸易、检疫及其他相关事宜。虽然种植棉花的农民表示他们通过轧棉厂商的种植计划得到优质种子，但花生行业在这方面仍存在问题。种植花生的农民表示，他们使用主要是从非正规渠道获得的回收种子，所以政策没有得到有效的实施。虽然国家农业政策通过提供研究的种畜/种子为非正规种子行业的发展创造条件，但调查结果显示，由于缺乏分拣的技术能力，农民无法根据花生的品种和档次进行分拣。另外，种植花生的农民都不愿意采用新改良品种，这可能是由于信息不对称导致的，因而需要组织关于使用能够提高产量的新改良品种方面的基层培训项目，并扩展推广服务。这也需要开设省级的"种子银行"。此政策的实施对于上述问题的解决将有很大助益。

　　国家农业政策将农民团体、农民田间学校、使用电子和印刷媒体作为传播工具以支持推广服务方面的信息传递作为战略性举措，但仍未付诸实施。

6 总结与建议

正如本研究指出的，农民表示，推广服务人员在一年内只来访了 3 次，在铜带省、东部省和南部省分别只有约 71%、78% 和 84% 接受采访的农民表示他们有机会获得推广服务。地方农业协调员证实了这一点，将其归因于人手不足。显而易见，政策的实施需要得到加强，使更多的人获得推广服务。为了提供有效的推广服务，需要足够的人员配置，提高业务效率。为增加推广服务的覆盖面，需要地方农业协调办公室在每方圆 10 千米的范围内设立一个分支机构。

国家农业政策也尚未解决资金方面的问题，尽管国家农业政策的确提议成立一个基金会，使农民能够通过适宜的金融机构获得资金，并鼓励集体贷款。所有接受采访的农民都表示，他们无缘获得金融机构提供的计划贷款，这是由于在赞比亚的借贷成本高、不利于小农生产者所导致的。因此，建议政府根据国家农业政策，开始采取措施，保证小规模农民获得贷款。政府应通过合作制度和鼓励建立自助团体来促进提供小额贷款。需要鼓励私营部门投资农业，而政府发挥监管的作用。

此外，虽然国家农业政策承诺采取措施，促进市场信息在各地区利益相关方之间的流动，包括促进农村基础设施建设，如道路、农村的存储基础设施、发展市场中心等，但小农仍然面临市场营销方面的问题。花生行业的营销渠道基本上是非正规的。调查结果还显示，三省农民使用的存储设施落后，导致了收获后的损失。在病虫害防治方面，记录保存和消防安全举措也存在问题。在畜牧行业，农民面临的问题源于他们没有冷藏设施（政府应采取措施并鼓励私人投资建设存储设施），这使小农户难以连续性地生产山羊肉和牛肉。因此，国家农业政策在市场营销方面的措施迫切需要贯彻实施。在实施中，有必要建立省级召集中心/信息单元，也有必要开设能力建设工作坊，传播关于国家及其他重要利益相关方的市场信息。

灌溉政策方面也存在政策执行不力的现象。虽然更新了灌溉工程规划、设计和建设方面的标准和指导原则，以惠及小农生产者，但这些仍未开始大规模地付诸实施。事实上，在铜带省、东部省和南省，分别约有 76%、62% 和 50% 的农民没有进行任何形式的灌溉，这一现象令人担忧。正如前面提到的，有必要促进灌溉政策的实施，以提高小农的生产力。

由国家合作社发展政策制定的策略也将提高小农的生产能力。发展法规和制度体系，以促进合作组织的重新定位和改革，通过工作人员实地直接处理合作社方面的问题，保证农牧业部在全国所有地区切实承担起在合作社发展方面的责任。如果要促进发展赞比亚的山羊养殖，应鼓励发展合作养殖，以保证农民的收益。考虑到人员配置和运营效率方面的问题，需要重构现有的合作组织。

农民也有必要转变观念。所有的农民都表示，他们让山羊自己寻找食物，没有正规的喂养计划。牛肉生产也是一样，投入在很大程度上依赖于传统的牧场。有必要为小规模农户指明方向，并帮助他们提高技能，使其认识到山羊和肉牛的养殖需要进行投入。政府的支持对提高生产力将起到很大推动作用。

本研究也证实，即便在农业部门的投资受到欢迎，仍有必要鼓励私营部门参与技术方面的投资。需要对一些问题予以关注，以保证投资符合"负责任农业投资原则"。有必要保证现有的对土地及相关自然资源的权利得到承认和尊重，保证农户不会在违背其意愿的情况下失去土地。在征收农民的土地时，需要保证告知当事人所有的信息。被迁移农户在新投资的区域占地过少的情况也许意味着投资危及粮食安全，基于农民的生产低于投资前的情况，应采取进一步的措施，保证征询所有因大型投资而蒙受物质损失的当事人的意见，记录并履行协商达成的协议。

另外一个明显存在的问题是农民土地所有权制度的薄弱。报告中指出，土地所有权的主要形式是传统的土地所有权，只有37.5%的受访者表示拥有土地所有权契据。其中70%来自铜带省，一个以城市为主的省份。土地所有权契据对农民获得贷款有很大的帮助，因为它可以用来作为抵押品。我们需要重新审视土地所有权制度，以保证更多的农民拥有土地的土地所有权契据。

参考文献

阿斯兰·阿斯里汉等：《应对农业土地争夺》，《基尔政策简报》第31期，2011年6月。

齐沙拉：《赞比亚农业技术传播状况分析》，南非发展共同体，2007。

《第六次赞比亚国家发展计划，2011~2015，公民社会视角（2010）》，赞比亚民间减贫组织，2010。

J. 法林顿、O. 萨萨：《赞比亚农业改革的驱动力：辨析塑造政策环境的因素》，英国国际发展署，2002。

《灌溉政策（2004）》，赞比亚农牧业部，2004。

《国家农业政策（2004~2015）》，赞比亚农牧业部，2004。

《国家合作发展政策（2011）》，赞比亚农牧业部，2011。

《国家种子产业政策（1999）》，赞比亚农牧业部，1999。

凯琳达·汤姆森等：《土地利用综合评估数据在赞比亚农林政策评估与分析中的运用》，联合国粮食及农业组织，2008。

《粮价飞涨下的赞比亚国家行动计划》，联合国粮食及农业组织，2009年5月。

尼古拉斯·J. 席塔克等：《技术纲要：对赞比亚农业的描述性统计与分析——基于美国国际开发署代表团"保障未来粮食供给战略评估"》，食品安全研究项目52号工作文件，2011年4月。

尼古拉斯·J. 席塔克等：《在赞比亚通过电子凭证制度实施"农民投入支持项目"的可行性评估》，印达巴农业政策研究所第53期政策简报，2012年4月。

《农作物预测调查2011/2012》，赞比亚农牧业部，2012。

《贫瘠土地治理系统下的大规模农业投资：赞比亚案例中的参与者与组织机构》，世界银行土地与贫困年度会议论文，华盛顿：世界银行，2012年4

月 23～26 日。

《赞比亚人口健康调查》，赞比亚中央统计办公室，2007。

《赞比亚投资政策评估》，经济合作与发展组织，2012。

《赞比亚人类发展报告》，联合国开发计划署，2011。

Assessment of the Status of the Zambia's Agriculture Sector Development Framework and Its Impacts and Contribution to Improvement of Small Scale Producers' Livelihoods

Contents

Executive Summary / 51

1. Background / 56
    1. 1 Problem statement / 57
    1. 2 Rationale for study / 58
    1. 3 Research objectives / 58
    1. 4 Methodology / 59

2. Overview of Zambia agriculture sector / 63
    2. 1 Evolution of the sector / 64
    2. 2 Participation of small scale farmers / 65
        2. 2. 1 Engagement in key agriculture activities / 65
        2. 2. 2 Contribution of small scale producers to production / 66
        2. 2. 3 Gender dynamics / 67
    2. 3 Key performance indicators / 67
        2. 3. 1 Contribution of Agriculture to National Income / 67
        2. 3. 2 Contribution to Poverty Reduction / 68

2.3.3 Contribution to Food Security and Nutritional Status / 70

3. Policy and Institutional framework to enhance small scale production / 71

3.1 Policy Framework / 71

3.1.1 National Agriculture policy (2004 – 2015) / 71

3.1.2 Irrigation policy (2004) / 75

3.1.3 National Seed Industry Policy (1999) / 79

3.1.4 National Cooperative Development Policy (2011) / 81

3.2 Institutional framework / 83

3.3 Implementation strategies / 85

4. Agriculture investment / 88

5. Fieldwork findings / 95

5.1 Input side / 95

5.1.1 Access to Land / 95

5.1.2 Access to Irrigation / 96

5.1.3 Access to Extension/ Inputs / 98

5.1.4 Access to Credit / 100

5.1.5 Access to Veterinary Services / 101

5.1.6 Access to Closest Permanent Road / 102

5.2 Output side / 103

5.3 Marketing issues / 105

6. Conclusions and recommendations / 108

References / 113

Executive Summary

Although the government of Zambia and other stakeholders have been running different programmes and projects to facilitate and create a conducive environment to graduate farmers from small scale to medium scale producers, this has still remained a pipe dream for the country. It is undeniable that the agriculture sector is the pillar for the country's rural economy; this means that growth in the agricultural sector is the clearest avenue through which poverty reduction can be achieved in Zambia. Notwithstanding the widespread recognition of the strong connection between agricultural development and poverty reduction, there is continuing under – provision of public investments for over a decade. Mostly, the constraints caused by the under – provision of public investments have highly affected the small scale farmers hence inhibiting their capacity to commercialise their production. The study assessed whether the status of the Zambia's Agriculture Sector Development Framework is adequate enough to allow the small farmers graduate to medium scale and hence improve their livelihoods.

The study reveals that Zambia has great potential to increase agricultural production immensely, as it is highly endowed in land, labour and water. Zambia has total land area of 75 million hectares, for which 58 percent is classified as medium to high potential for agricultural production, given rainfall patterns ranging between 800mm to 1400mm annually. Zambia land is also suitable for the production of a broad range of crops, fish, and livestock. From total land area, FAO estimates that only 14 percent of total agricultural land is currently being utilized.

Despite this immense potential, Zambia farmers face several challenges, which include lack of access to affordable credit, extension service, veterinary services,

Assessment of the Status of the Zambia's Agriculture Sector Development Framework and Its Impacts and Contribution to Improvement of Small Scale Producers' Livelihoods

good transport and storage infrastructure, and lack of access to a readily available market among others. There is enough evidence to indicate that the most hit by these constraints are the small scale farmers. It is interesting to note that 70 percent of the farmers are small scale farmers and they have greater opportunities to be fully involved in the agriculture growth framework, given Zambia's conducive rainfall patterns and soil fertility. The agriculture sector has the potential to become a bigger engine of economic growth in Zambia. It is regrettable to note that despite several government and donor funded programmes, small scale farmers have failed to graduate to medium scale farmers, due to the fact that essential factors to exacerbate growth among the small scale farmers still remain underdeveloped.

This study established there is still a lot of room for the agriculture sector to develop faster, especially if more attention is devoted to the small scale farmers. They account for more than 70 percent of the farmers and dominate the growing of maize, millet, sorghum, groundnuts and cotton in terms of crop production. The study has identified some issues that need urgent attention to ensure that small scale farmers' productivity is enhanced. Addressing several challenges such as lack of access to affordable credit, extension service, veterinary services, poor transport and storage infrastructure, and access to a readily available market among others could help in uplifting the lives of farmers. These are the major constraints facing the farmers in general but those operating at a small scale level are most hit. The existing policy framework does however note these challenges although the remedies to these challenges are yet to be put in place.

Zambia's agricultural development framework is governed by theNational Agriculture Policy (NAP). NAP provides for a framework which sets out the tenets to follow in advancing agriculture; hence analysing this policy was essential for this research. For example, NAP provides that there would be regularisation of the seed sector through seed testing, seed crop inspection, variety registration, variety protection and enforcement of seed quality standards to facilitate seed trade, quarantine and other seed related issues. Although cotton farmers indicated that they receive quality seeds, the groundnut sector still has challenges as farmers still use recycled seeds. Although the NAP provides for the development of the informal seed sector by providing accessibility of the sector to breeders/basic seed from research, findings reveal that farmers are unable to sort groundnuts according to varieties and grades due to lack of capacity in sorting techniques.

The NAP also recognises the need for an effective and efficient extension and information system in the country. However, the study notes that there is need to build capacity in terms of adequate staffing and operation efficiency, and increasing access to extension services, which requires the office of the DACOs to open sub branches in every 10 km radius.

The NAP is also yet to deal with the issue of access to finance, despite noting the need to create a fund to encourage group lending. Thus it is recommended that the government should promote the provision of Micro finance through cooperative system and establishment of self help groups should be encouraged.

In addition, although NAP promises strategies that facilitate market information flow among stakeholders in various regions, including facilitating the provision of rural infrastructure such as roads, rural storage infrastructure and developing market centres, marketing is still a challenge for small scale farmers. Thus the provisions on marketing in the NAP call for urgent implementation.

Implementation gaps are also apparent in the irrigation policy. Although updating the standards and guidelines for the planning, design and construction of irrigation schemes to benefit small scale farmers are part of the strategies, this is yet to commence on a large scale. It is recommended that that productivity of small scale farmers can be increased if farmers use alternative sources of irrigation such as installation of pumps, have provisions of harvesting rain water and it's storage and also have suitable ground governance programme implemented by stakeholder.

Another policy that was looked at in the study was the Cooperative Development Policy. This Policy identifies strategies identified to enhance the performance of small scale farmers. The development of a legal and institutional framework to facilitate the re – orientation and reforming of the co – operative organisation and ensuring that the Ministry responsible for cooperatives has a physical presence in all the districts of the country through field staff directly dealing with co – operative matters is one strategy which this study sees as a positive recommendation. Cooperative farming should be encouraged to ensure productive returns to the farmers.

One specific sub – sector which the study focuses on is goat production and trade. The study observes that the main challenge for farmers involved in goat business hinged on attitude. Change in attitude to make goat raring a mainstream business need to be encouraged as the use of free scavenging methods to feed the goats, with no formalised feeding schemes is common. The same is true for beef production. The need therefore is to orient and build capacity of small scale farmers to treat both goat and beef farming as a business for extra revenue for re – investment in social and economic aspects at household and community level.

The study has also established that although investment into the agriculture sector is welcome, there are also some issues that need attention to ensure that the investment is in line with the PRAI. There is need to ensure that the existing rights to land and associated natural resources are recognized and respected by ensuring that some households do not lose land against their will. The study also recommends ensuring that full information is disclosed to the farmers when land is being acquired as a way of respecting rights to land. The study further observes that in instances low uptake by the displaced farmers in newly invested areas might imply that the investment is jeopardizing food security as farmers' production would become lower than the situation before the investment.

Lastly, the study also notes the challenge of a weak land tenure system among the farmers. As found out in the report, the predominant form of land ownership is customary land ownership, with only 37.5 percent of the respondents indicating that they had title deeds. Among these, about 70 percent were from Copperbelt province, an urban province. Having title deeds would go a long way in helping the farmers to unlock credit, as these could be used as collateral.

1

Background

The agriculture sector is one of the priority sectors earmarked to leverage the achievement of sustainable economic development in Zambia. It shoulders a great deal of economic burden of the country with most of the country's problems directly or indirectly linked to the performance of the sector. Its versatile roles range from economic and social development to food security through foreign exchange generation, rural development and poverty reduction. Recent data indicate that the sector is underdeveloped and has been growing at about 4 percent, which is below the 6 percent recommended growth rate under the Comprehensive African Agriculture Development Programme (CAADP), (UNDP, 2011). Just like the Maputo declaration of 2003, the CAADP requires African governments to invest at least 10 percent of their national budgets in the agriculture sector to achieve the set target annual growth rate of at least 6 percent. Although it is underdeveloped, the sector remains one of the largest employers accounting for over 70 percent of the total labour force, with over 80 percent of the people living in rural areas dependent on the sector. Its contribution to the Gross Domestic Product (GDP) stands at about 21 percent but trails behind services and extractive sectors (MAL, 2012). The country's policy and development frameworks identify the agriculture sector as one of the potential economic drivers.

For the agriculture sector to effectively meet its objective in Zambia, it has to be fully developed with emphasis placed on small scale farmers and producers who are the majority and continue to be impoverished. Targeting small – scale agricultural systems is critical and this should be done through new and innovative public – private partnerships, increased public and private investments in research (related to increasing productivity) and extension systems, and development – oriented local governance and institutions. Further, addressing generic constraints such as irrigation and water challenges, capacity, productivity, storage, market intelligence and access, transport systems etc, is essential in advancing the performance of the sector. All these are recognised in the overall agricultural development framework for Zambia. It is therefore important to assess theextent to which Zambia's Development Framework is helping small farmers and producers to improve their livelihood.

1.1 Problem statement

As agriculture provides the main support for Zambia's rural economy, growth in the agricultural sector is the clearest avenue through which poverty reduction can be achieved in Zambia. However, despite widespread recognition of the strong connection between agricultural development and poverty reduction, there is continuing under – provision of public investments for over a decade and small scale farmers have continued to wallow in poverty for a very long period. Zambia's primary policy objective of achieving accelerated growth and competitiveness in the agricultural sector cannot be achieved unless adequate public resources are committed towards catalyzing the desired growth. Long – term public investment in research and development, extension services, rural infrastructure, and food safety and quality systems have high pay – offs and are among the most important drivers of agricultural growth and competitiveness. Mostly, it's the small scale farmers who are highly affected by the challenges inhibiting the commercialisation of their production. In this regard, there is a need to understand the extent to which Zambia's agriculture development framework is involving and helping small farmers and producers to improve their production and eventually their livelihood.

1.2 Rationale for study

The Zambia agriculture sector comprises mainly of the small scale farmers in the rural areas facing different obstacles to participate fully in the agriculture growth framework. Despite the government and NGOs establishingand implementing different programmes to create a conducive environment to graduate farmers from small scale to medium scale producers in terms of their production and productivity, this has still remained a pipe dream for the country. The study is therefore important as it would assess whether the status of the Zambia's Agriculture Sector Development Framework is adequate enough while providing recommendations to improve the implementation of the framework.

1.3 Research objectives

The objectives of the study include the following:
- Investigate the Zambia agriculture growth framework in terms of policies, nature of growth and how its supports poverty reduction, key sectors, and levels of investment both public and private;
- Investigate what policy constraints are impacting negatively on small scale farmers particularly women;
- Identify and analyse the engagement and contribution of small scale producers, in terms of nature of contribution, size, and the extent to which the sector is contributing to poverty reduction, paying specific attention to women farmers;
- Analyse specific opportunities that exist for smallholder involvement in the growth framework and identify existing constraints blocking their full involvement;
- Analyse profiles of good public private partnerships – practices and policies and how poor producers are engaged in assessing these partnerships; alternative or

potential areas for investment that may be more effective in livelihoods improvement and poverty reduction;

• Assess how the current agriculture development framework impacts the community of poor producers, in the immediate and in the long term. This should be viewed from the point of view of access to markets and services, resources and, implications for farming for food;

• Analyse the performance of the agriculture sector against agreed targets like the Comprehensive African Agriculture Development Programme (CAADP) framework.

1.4 Methodology

The study made an assessment on agriculture sub – markets at three levels; the input, output and market side, defined as follows:

• Input side; include among others issues related to access to credit; access to seed varieties, and fertiliser; access to water or irrigation (how public and private investment are playing their role), extension services (how effective and functional is this service facility); access to quality feed, access to quality pasture and water, access to timely and quality veterinary services etc.

• Output side; include among others post – harvest facilities for preservation and storage, transport infrastructure, marketing and the kind of marketing institutions.

• Market; include among others availability of a market for particular products, market intelligence among small scale farmers, existing uncompetitive practices at supply level and how they are being addressed etc,

Three crops were selected for detailed analysis under the study, with the selection criteria being (a) the crops which are among the major crops in terms of hectarage and (b) crops which are dominated by small scale farmers in their production since the study is aimed at improving livelihoods of small scale producers. The crops selected were maize, cotton and groundnuts, based on the findings of the crop forecast survey for 2011/2012. The study also selected goat and beef production for detailed assessment from the livestock side, given that this is where the bulk of small scale farmers are concentrated in the livestock subsector.

To assess whether any alternative or potential areas for investment exist that may be more effective in livelihoods improvement, CUTS assessed foreign investment that has been received into the sector over the years. In particular, the assessment was done taking into cognisance the level of both foreign and local investment across the three stages for all the three crops and livestock. The Principles of Responsible Agricultural Investments (PRAI), developed by FAO, IFAD, UNCTAD and the World Bank were observed as the basis for the assessment. The principles that were found relevant for the study include the following;

- Principle 1: *Existing rights to land and associated natural resources are recognized and respected.*
- Principle 2: *Investments do not jeopardize food security but rather strengthen it.*
- Principle 3: *Processes relating to investment in agriculture are transparent, monitored, and ensure accountability by all stakeholders, within a proper business, legal, and regulatory environment.*
- Principle 4: *All those materially affected are consulted, and agreements from consultations are recorded and enforced.*
- Principle 5: *Investors ensure that projects respect the rule of law, reflect industry best practice, are viable economically, and result in durable shared value.*
- Principle 6: *Investments generate desirable social and distributional impacts and do not increase vulnerability.*
- Principle 7: *Environmental impacts of a project are quantified and measures taken to encourage sustainable resource use, while minimizing the risk/magnitude of negative impacts and mitigating them.*

The inputs to unpack the above issues would be obtained through both primary and secondary data as follows:

Secondary data analysis

This involved evaluating available policies and their synergies both at policy and implementation level and assessing whether the policies had the necessary provisions to promote agriculture at the three stages in the value chain. The National Agriculture Policy together with other sub – market policies was the basis for the analysis.

Primary data

In order to gather first hand information, the study also used primary data. Primary data collection instruments included both structured questions used to collect information from key informants and structured questionnaires administered to a selected sample. Structured questions were used to interview senior level officials in key institutions that are stakeholders in the agriculture sector. These included District Agricultural Coordinators' offices, Agricultural Consultative Forum, Livestock Development Trust, Indaba agricultural Policy Research Institute, ZNFU, Beef Association of Zambia, ZDA and Cotton Association of Zambia.

Structured questionnaires were administered to get ground realities across towns and districts, which saw a sample of 120 farmers being interviewed to gather their views and experiences. Among these, 40 farmers were from the Copperbelt Province, 40 were from the Eastern Province while 40 were from the Southern Province. Southern province is a province with a lot of potential for goat and beef production by small scale farmers, with such potential currently not fully utilized. Copperbelt is an urban province which is starting to take off in agricultural growth in the recent years after traditionally being dominated by mining. The Eastern Province is a province which is mainly characterised by small scale farmers and is performing very well in cotton, groundnuts and maize production as compared to other province, in addition it is also performing well in beef and goat production. This can be attested by the crop forecast survey of 2011/2012.

Analysis of Data

After the completion of the field work the data and information collected was analysed and presented at a stakeholder workshop.

Limitation of the Study

This study was not allocated enough time. This meant that very little time was given to interview different stakeholders. This also meant some of the important stakeholders were not interviewed. Access to certain information was also a challenge as some of the data that was crucial was not recorded by responsible institutions, for instance the contribution of individual crops and livestock to the agricultural contribution to GDP.

Overview of Zambia agriculture sector

Zambia is a country that has a great potential to increase agricultural production immensely, as it is highly endowed in terms of land, labour and water. Zambia has total land area of 75 million hectares, for which 58 percent is classified as medium to high potential for agricultural production, given rainfall patterns ranging between 800mm to 1400mm annually. Zambia's land is also suitable for the production of a broad range of crops, fish, and livestock. It is estimated that only 14 percent of total agricultural land is currently being utilized (FAO, 2008). Zambia has one of the best surface and underground water resources in Southern Africa, with many rivers, lakes, and dams. In addition to this, Zambia's high potential underground water aquifers in many areas offers excellent prospects for irrigation programmes although these water bodies are highly unexploited. Although the country's irrigation potential conservatively is estimated at 423000 hectares, only about 50000 hectares are currently irrigated, implying that the resources are underutilized (FAO, 2008).

Zambia is a country that is that is subdivided in three agro ecological regions on the basis of rainfall patterns. Zone I is characterised by low rainfall, short growing season, high temperatures during the growing season, and a high risk of drought. Zone III is characterised by high rainfall, long growing season, low probability of drought, and cooler temperatures during the growing season. Zone II falls in between Zone I and III for most climatic variables (Saasa and Farrigton, 2002). There are great variations in the agronomic features (rainfall, elevation, mean temperatures, vegetation and soils) among the three zones. Zone I is found in the main valleys of Zambia such as the Luangwa Valley in Eastern Zambia and the Gwembe Valley in the south. It also encompasses parts of Western and Southern Provinces. Zone II is mainly found in the central parts of the country, i. e. Central, Eastern, Lusaka and Southern Provinces and some parts of Western Province. The northern parts of the country consisting of Northern, Luapula, Copperbelt and Northwestern Provinces lie in Region III.

2.1 Evolution of the sector

The economic policy changes that have been introduced over the years have had an impact on the evolution of the agriculture sector in Zambia. Table 1 shows an outline of the policy changes in chronological order. These changes have led to the evolution of the way the agriculture sector is being operated in Zambia. In the first regime, there was a controlled economy, where the government offered all the inputs, services and a ready market for the farmers. The farmers became over dependent on the government for production and marketing of the produce.

In 1991 the government introduced a fully fledged structural adjustment programme, which meant that the economy had moved from a command economy to a liberalised one. This meant that the farmers had to fend for themselves with regards to inputs and the marketing of their produce. This transition for farmers was very difficult and thus led to a reduction in the national's total agriculture production.

In 2001, the government decided to set agriculture as a priority and came up with the National Agricultural Policy (2004 – 2015) which brought in programmes that stimulated growth in the agriculture sector.

2 Overview of Zambia agriculture sector

Table 1   Chronology of Zambia's economic policy changes

Before December 1982	Centralised planning and controlled regime
December 1982 – October 1985	Decontrols and deregulation
October 1985 – April 1987	Highly liberalised regime
May 1987 – November 1988	Return to controlled regime
November 1988 – June 1989	Relaxation of some controls
July 1989 – November 1991	Towards full – scale liberalisation
November 1991 – December 2001	Fully – fledged Structural Adjustment Programme
December 2001 – Present	(a) Guarded approach to liberation/privatisation (b) the re – introduction of national planning and (c) the development of National Development Plans

Source: *Farrington & Saasa*, 2002.

2.2   Participation of small scale farmers

2.2.1   Engagement in key agriculture activities

Most of the farmers in the rural areas are small scale farmers who largely produce for subsistence and sustenance of their livelihood. The agriculture sector can be improved by the small holders if the government puts a deliberate policy to create an enabling environment for small scale farmers to diversify, improve productivity and target accessible markets.

The opportunities for small scale farmers' engagement in the agriculture growth framework are very immense, given Zambia's conducive rainfall patterns and soil fertility. Agriculture has the potential to become a bigger engine of economic growth in Zambia mostly by increasing GDP per capitaand reducing poverty levels in the rural communities. Despite this vast potential to produce and increase sales by the farmers, the agriculture sector still remains under developed. Different government and donor funded programmes have failed to graduate small scale farmers into medium scale farmers in terms of their production and productivity, due to the fact that essential factors to exacerbate growth among the small scale farmers still remain underdeveloped. Only until Zambia manages to ease the access to inputs, training and extension services, post – harvest management and markets to the small scale farmers will we see noticeable growth. In addition to this, the government should provide for the needed infrastructure (feeder roads among others) to facilitate the reduction of cost in farming among the rural community.

2.2.2 Contribution of small scale producers to production

It is evident that small scale farmers are the majority in the farming cycles, they account for more than 70 percent of the farmers involved in agriculture. According to the crop forecast survey of 2011/2012, these small holder farmers have dominated the farming of maize, millet, sorghum, groundnuts, cotton accounting for 95, 99.9, 93, 99.5 and 99.4 percent respectively in terms of crop production, which proves that the small scale farmers are contributing substantially to the entire agricultural production. This assertion can be amplified by looking at the maize subsector keeping in mind that it's a staple crop for Zambia. The table below indicates the contribution of both the large and small scale farmers towards maize production.

Table 2   Contribution of farmers (metric tonnes) by category to maize production

Maize Production	2002/03	2003/04	2004/05	2005/06	2006/07	2007/08	2008/09
Large scale	412381	253861	254804	313519	287089	218728	229893
Small scale	745479	959740	611382	1110919	1079069	992838	1657117
Total Production	1157861	1213601	866187	1424439	1366158	1211566	1887010
Large Scale % Contribution	36	21	29	22	21	18	12

Source: SNDP, *A Civil Society Perspective*, 2010.

The table above indicates that the contribution of large scale farmers towards maize production has been declining continuously from 36 percent in 2002/2003 period to 12 percent in 2008/2009 season. This is an indication that the small scale farmers are the ones feeding the nation and their contribution to agriculture is very significant.

2.2.3 Gender dynamics

The agriculture sector is a major employer with 49 percent and 48 percent of the employed being women and men respectively (CSPR, 2010). Conversely, most women (55 percent) that are employed in the agriculture sector are not paid for their labour (ZDHS, 2007). Women are responsible for the 80 percent of food production and provide about 80 percent of the labour in subsistence farmers (CSPR, 2010). Despite the involvement of more women in agriculture production, they experience limited access to technology, credit, extension services and inputs. This can be reaffirmed by the lesser participation of female farmer in the Farmers Input Support Programme (FISP). Gender dynamics need to be addressed consciously in order to allow maximum economic growth and poverty reduction in the rural areas.

Table 3 Poverty Status of Household Headed by men and women in Percent, 2006

Gender	Total poor	Extremely poor	Non poor	Population
Male Headed	63	49	34	9395704
Female Headed	70	57	29	2289327
Whole country	64	51	32	11685031

Source: *UNDP Human Development report for Zambia*, 2011.

Keeping in mind that much of employment in Zambia is in the agriculture sector, Table 3 above clearly indicates that female-headed households continue to experience the highest levels of poverty.

2.3 Key performance indicators

2.3.1 Contribution of Agriculture to National Income

As can be seen from the Figure 1, the agriculture has been contributing positively to the national income though it has been quite static (about 21 percent). It is really a concern that despite the country experiencing good rainfall in the recent past, the performance has not been consistent. However, the country experienced bumper harvest in 2010 and 2011.

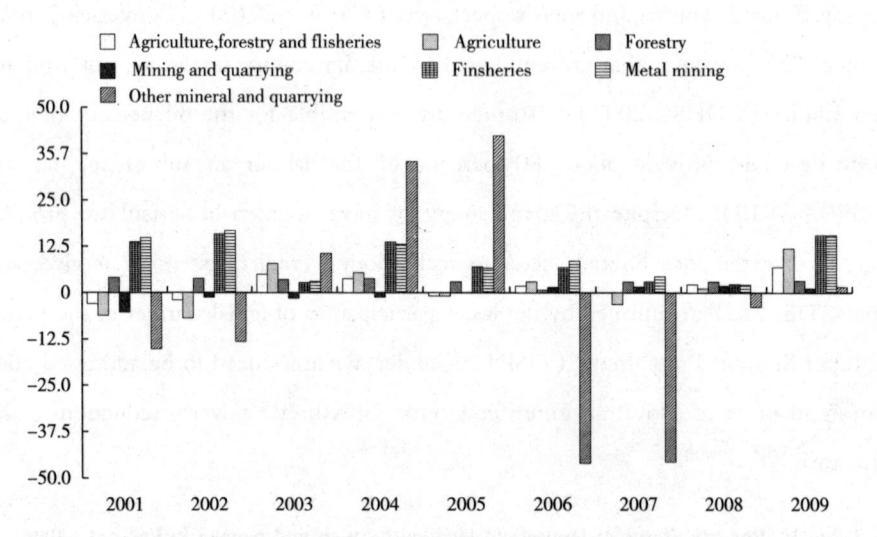

Figure 1 Percentage contribution to real GDP by sub–sector
Source: *UNDP Human Development Report for Zambia*, 2011.

2.3.2 Contribution to Poverty Reduction

Aagriculture has been earmarked in the Sixth National Development Plan as a key sector that should be used for sustainable economic growth and eventually to reduce poverty levels in the country. Having sustained growth in the agriculture sector will facilitate the farmers to enjoy better incomes, and hence have an improved livelihood.

Despite the agriculture sector being a positive contributor to the national income, the poverty levels still remain high as can be attested by UNDP Human Development report for Zambia, 2011 which indicated that:

• 58.3 percent of the Zambian population lived in poor households in 2006, compared to 56.3 percent in 2004;

- the average poor person was deprived in 44 percent of the weighted indicators in 2006, compared to 42. 8 percent in 2004;
- the share of the population that is multi dimensionally poor[①] (adjusted by the intensity of the deprivations suffered) was 0. 257 in 2006, compared to 0. 241 in 2004.

This shows that the agriculture sector has not performed very well due to its failure to significantly create employment opportunities that can be mirrored by high poverty levels, especially in rural areas, where most people derive their incomes from farming. This is an indication that there is a lot that is needed to be done in order to improve the rate of equitable growth for the Zambian economy.

Table 4 Breakdown of allocations under the poverty reduction programmes by percent, 2006 – 2011

Category	2006	2007	2008	2009	2010
Irrigation support	0. 7	2. 4	2	1	0. 1
Commercialization of farm blocks	2. 2	2. 6	2. 2	0	0
Animal disease control	1. 5	1. 6	3. 3	4. 2	2. 5
Livestock development	0	0. 9	0. 6	0. 6	0. 4
Fertilizer Support Programme	74	38. 2	62. 2	75. 6	78
Strategic Food Reserves	18. 6	52. 1	26. 9	17. 4	18. 1
Cooperative education and training	0. 3	0. 7	0. 2	0	0
Others	2. 2	0. 7	2. 7	0	0. 9
Total	100	99. 2	100. 1	98. 8	100
Total ZK billion	198. 8	196	198. 2	196. 6	199. 9

Source: *Agricultural Consultative Forum/Food Security Research Project* 2006 – 2010.

Table 4 above illustrates that on average the allocation to poverty reduction programmes (Irrigation Support, Land Development, FISP among other items detailed in the table above) have maintained an upward trend between 2006 and

---

[①] Multi dimensionally poor index (MPI) is a measure that identifies multiple deprivations at the individual level in health, education and standard of living.

2010. Much of the allocation went to FISP and Strategic Food Reserves which when combined in the year 2010, it accounts for 92.1 percent while the five others remaining with 7.4 percent.

In analyzing the same table above, UNDP Human Development report for Zambia, 2011 indicated that the skewed distribution of the poverty reduction allocations were reduced on services such as irrigation and support for livestock production. Although the country has experienced growth in the production of maize, this may have come at the cost of increased inequality, since pricing policies may represent a *de facto* transfer of rent from the maize – consuming population to the big commercial farmers. This UNDP report also indicated that areas critical for enhancing productivity, such as crop science, extension programmes, infrastructure development, and a stable and supportive policy environment have not received the needed support.

2.3.3　Contribution to Food Security and Nutritional Status

The UNDP human development report clearly indicated that the recent gains in crop production (bumper harvest) Zambia has experienced have been matched with improved food security, at least at the macro – level. On the other hand, the micro – level food security is however dependent on other factors, such as rural household involvement in food and non – food crop production, the inclination to export and the gender distribution of power at the household level. In Zambia, these factors have combined to make micro – level food insecurity a major concern (UNDP human development report, 2011).

One of the indicators of the food and nutritional status of the population is the food poverty headcount. Food poverty is not only higher than overall poverty but has declined a great deal more slowly than over the past years (UNDP, 2011). This implies that while the overall poverty fell by 8.8 percent between 1996 and 2006, food poverty only fell by 6.3 percent between 1996 and 2006 (UNDP human development report, 2011).

Policy and Institutional framework to enhance small scale production

3.1 Policy Framework

It is important to analyse the existing policy framework to assess whether they have the necessary provisions to promote agriculture at the three stages in the value chain (i.e input side, output side and marketing stage), especially with a view to assessing whether small scale producers would benefit from these interventions. The following are some of the critical policies which shape the Zambia agriculture sector.

3.1.1 National Agriculture policy (2004 –2015)

The overall objective of the National Agriculture Policy is to facilitate and support the development of a sustainable and competitive agricultural sector that assures food security in Zambia. In pursuit of this objective, the following constitute its specific objectives:

- To ensure national and household food security through an all – year round production and post – harvest management of adequate supplies of basic foodstuffs at competitive costs;
- To contribute to sustainable industrial development by providing locally produced agro – based raw materials;

- To increase agricultural exports thereby enhancing the sector's contribution to the National Balance of Payments;

- To generate income and employment through increased agriculture production and productivity; and

- To ensure that the existing agricultural resource base is maintained and improved upon.

The policy has provisions that affect the manner in which agriculture activities are conducted at the three stages. At the input stage, one of the provisions aims at preventing and controlling pests, crop and livestock diseases. To achieve this, the policy provides that the monitoring, regulation and facilitation of disease and vector control implementation programmes for diseases of economic importance would be intensified in priority areas. Ensuring that the crops and livestock are protected against diseases is critical as this affects the extent to which agriculture activities could turn out to be productive. Thus key inputs towards these identified by the policy include the making available pesticides and veterinary medicine. Besides, the policy also seeks development and promotion of the use of plant and herbal – based veterinary medicine.

The promotion of irrigation is also a key strategy identified under the policy which would help transform agriculture at the input stage. Given that reduced crop yields and livestock losses in Zambia can also be attributed to severe droughts suffered from time to time, the policy provides for Government to embark on full and efficient exploitation of the country's abundant water resources, both underground and surface, and promoting irrigation to ensure all year round agricultural production. This is particularly with reference to small – scale farmers, who would be prioritised to improve household food security and incomes.

The policy also has critical provisions aimed at ensuring that seed availability is enhanced in crop production. Of particular importance is the fact that the measures identified by the policy would help in ensuring the availability of both formal and informal sources of seed. The policy provides that there would be regularisation of the seed sector through seed testing, seed crop inspection, variety registration, variety protection and enforcement of seed quality standards to facilitate seed trade, quarantine and other seed related issues. This provision is critical as it would help to ensure that the formal seed market continues to use seeds that are best suited to the local environmental conditions to improve yield.

The policy provides for the development of the informal seed sector by providing accessibility of the sector to breeders/basic seed from research. In addition, the policy hopes to co-ordinate the sector to build and create a sustainable cottage (rural) seed industry. This provision is very important given that many rural farmers rely on informal seed sources, which include the use of uncertified seeds saved from previous harvests, not subjected to any testing and variety controls. The measures under the policy would reduce overreliance on informal sources for seeds.

The policy also recognises the movements in technology towards genetically modified crops by providing for the regulation of the multiplication, trading and adoption of seeds of genetically modified crops. The fact that the use of genetically modified crops is not banned but regulated implies that there is scope for Zambia farmers to remain competitive in the international market. Genetically modified crops reduce the production costs for farmers as the maturing time for the crops would be quickened, hence such farmers would become competitive in the international market. However, there are concerns on the potential effect on health, which would justify the need for regulation as identified under the policy.

The policy also has provisions regulating farming activities. One key requirement for productivity is expertise and the policy recognises that most rural farmers lack the skills to exploit the prevailing market conditions to their advantage. Thus the policy identifies that the existence of an effective and efficient extension and informa-

> The NAP does not provide for the harmonisation and regulation of the provision of extension services by the private sector and NGOs

tion system is essential in influencing the development of agriculture in the country. Thus the policy aims at putting in place strategies that promote and strengthen farmer groups and farmer field schools as targets for technology transfer. This also includes the use of electronic and print media as communication tools to support extension information delivery.

The policy also acknowledges some limitations on the ability of government to provide extension services on its own. Thus the policy is also aimed at promoting and encouraging the involvement of the private sector and NGOs in the provision of extension services, although it does not include the harmonization and regulation of the provision of extension services by the private sector and NGOs. Other strategies to improve production include the promotion of crop diversification and use of improved technologies as well as facilitating delivery of skills training and technology transfer to small scale farmers using Farmer Training Institutes at staff level and Farmer Training Centres at farmer level.

The policy also recognises the importance of livestock farming and provides strategies to ensure that animal production is enhanced. This include the production and distribution of livestock training and extension materials/manuals for both farmers and field staff; regulating and controlling the quality of livestock, livestock products and stock feeds as well as promoting private sector participation in the provision of livestock and extension services, marketing of livestock and livestock products.

Access to finance remains one of the critical challenges for farmers. The policy provides for strategies in helping farmers to get access to funding. The Agriculture Policy also has some provisions on agriculture credit and finance. These include creating a fund for access by farmers through appropriate financial institutions and NGOs. In addition, the policy provides for the encouragement of group lending to ensure good recovery rates as well as the promotion of private/public sector partnership in credit provision and savings mobilization. If implemented, these provisions would go a long way in expanding agriculture output.

The policy also has some provisions to help in the marketing of agriculture produce. On marketing, the policy objective is to promote the development of a competitive, efficient and transparent public and private sector driven marketing system for agricultural commodities and inputs. In that regard, the policy aims at putting in place strategies that facilitate market information flow among stakeholders in various regions. The policy is also aimed at facilitating the provision of rural infrastructure such as roads, rural storage infrastructure and developing market centres. To encourage production, the policy is also aimed at providing guaranteed agricultural input and output markets, especially to small – scale farmers in rural areas. This also includes the promotion of crops with both domestic and export markets.

3.1.2　Irrigation policy (2004)

The overall objective of the Zambia irrigation policy is to have a well regulated and profitable irrigation sector that is attractive to both private investors and Zambia's development partners. This objective would be achieved through the addressing of a myriad of challenges, many of which have a bearing on small scale producers. For example, the policy notes that Zambia has a poorly enforced legal framework that neither regulates nor allocates water in an equitable or economically advantageous fashion hence making it difficult for small scale producers to actively participate in the system as they could benefit a lot from participating in irrigation farming if there is a good enforced legal framework for the policy in question.

In addition, the policy notes that there are challenges with respect to investment in the agriculture sector as there exists an administrative practice of issuing abstraction permits for short periods (on average five years), that discourages investment. Small scale producers could benefit if investment in the sector increases, as this would create markets for farmers due to increased demand for more agriculture products. Thus the extent to which the irrigation policy addresses the identified challenges would go a long way in benefiting the small scale producers.

To achieve the overall objective of having a well regulated and profitable irrigation sector, the irrigation policy also has some intermediate objectives that would help attain this main target. These include having accessible, demand – driven institutions characterized by efficient, transparent procedures and a service oriented ethos. One of the major challenges for small scale producers is the challenge in having access to institutions that readily respond to their needs. Thus if demand driven institutions are established, they would be largely those that would be able to respond to the demands from small scale producers as they constitute the majority of farmers in Zambia. The policy has also identified the existence of Zambia's market chain adding value to irrigated produce as an objective. One of the key challenges affecting productivity for small scale farmers are unclear market chains, as there are always challenges with the smooth transfer of agriculture produce across market chains. For example, perishable products could easily rot while markets are being explored, since the farming would have been carried out without the knowledge of alternative markets. The ability of the irrigation policy to address this challenge would go a long way in solving the plight of small scale farmers.

The strategies laid out under the irrigation policy can go a long way in uplifting the living standards of the small scale producers if successfully implemented. Although the policy has provided general strategies for all farmers, it also identifies three different categories of farmers and provides separate objective and strategies to attain them. General strategies for all farmers include re – aligning services required for the production and marketing of irrigated produce. If implemented, this would address many rigidities and bottlenecks in the agriculture sector related to marketing of produce. Another important strategy is the promotion of adaptive commercial credit mechanisms appropriate for the needs of existing and future private investors in irrigation. Ushering investment from private sector players is critical, given the limited fiscal space that government has. Under the policy, this would be done by identifying and removing market distortions while providing incentives for investment in added value opportunities. Easing government regulations on input costs as well as reviewing and revising the existing water tariff structure are also among the strategies. The only challenge with the policy is that it does not outline the specific strategies that would be put in place to attract private sector investment in irrigation, as well as how such investment could be made profitable.

The policy also identifies separate strategies for emerging farmers, which is where a significant proportion of commercial farmers is found. Although they are identified as less significant in terms of area than both commercial and traditional farmers, they are also considered very important since they represent the strategic stepping stone between traditional and commercial farmers. Challenges faced by these farmers identified under the policy include poor information and extension support; inadequate infrastructure; financing and organizational difficulties and highly exploitative, inequitable marketing lock – ins by rent seeking traders. Thus the use of improved irrigation technologies and services to expand the production base and productivity of the emerging farmers is identified as a key objective of the policy. To benefit these farmers, the policy aims at having improved access to irrigation inputs, technology, services and training and appropriate credit mechanisms for emerging farmers. This would be supported by strengthened regulatory mechanisms that ensure equitable access to goods and services for irrigated agricultural production. Strategies to achieve these include the following:

- Promoting irrigator organisations and developing an adaptable legal framework to recognise, protect and regulate such organisations and their members in a gender sensitive fashion;
- Specific provision in the water rights legislation that ensures equitable access by user groups as opposed to individuals;
- Identifying feasible modalities for transferring state schemes to emerging farmer groups and thereafter opening up state farms for emerging farmer use;
- Preparing information packs on production and processing of irrigated crops;

- Improving access to post – harvest and agro – processing advice and facilities;
- Establishing and enforcing a regulatory framework that protects emerging farmers from exploitation by middle men.

The irrigation policy also recognises traditional farmers, which are basically communal farmers engaged in subsistence farming with only the surplus being commercialised.

> The policy identifies the use of improved irrigation technologies and services can expand the production base and productivity of the emerging farmers

Irrigation in the context of traditional farmers would largely comprise public infrastructure in the form of minor canalisation, often supplied from small dams. However, many such infrastructures, which require largely public spending, remain dilapidated and unserviceable. Thus the overall objective of the policy with respect to traditional farmers is to empower them to develop and use irrigation and other water management technologies so as to alleviate poverty and achieve food security. In addition to the cross cutting strategies under the policy, strategies developed for traditional farmers include the promotion of a legal framework that regulates the establishment, legal status, structure and mandate of irrigator organizations and its members; updating the standards and guidelines for the planning, design and construction of irrigation schemes to include beneficiary consultation, sensitization and participation; rehabilitating and upgrading existing irrigation schemes. However, under the policy, the rehabilitation would only take place provided that there is strong demand from the user groups; user groups are thoroughly sensitised as to the level of participation expected and their responsibilities during, before and after commissioning of the works; and for works that are feasible. Such conditions might result in a lot of discretion on the policy implementers, which could disadvantage traditional farmers who do not have access to the required information to demand for the services.

Thus, just like the National Agriculture Policy, there is a lot of scope for the irrigation policy to benefit small scale and traditional farmers. There also remain some serious challenges that need to be addressed to make the policy more effective in achieving its enshrined objectives.

3.1.3 National Seed Industry Policy (1999)

As identified under the National Agriculture Policy, the availability of seed is critical, not only for the attainment of the policy targets but also for the attainment of food security in Zambia. In that regard, the National Seed Policy of Zambia was developed, whose overall policy objective is to ensure that quality seed of various crops is made available to farmers in an efficient and convenient manner to increase crop productivity and agricultural production. This would be achieved through the attainment of other intermediate objectives with benefit the small scale producers. These include ensuring the development of an effective, efficient and sustainable system of producing and supplying high quality seeds of crops to satisfy the national seed requirements. Given that shortage of seed, which results in high prices of seeds and high levels of use of traditional sources, is a major concern to farmers, implementation of this strategy would help in ensuring increased produce in Zambia.

The policy is also aimed at promoting an integrated seed industry involving both the formal and informal system. The recognition of the informal system in the seed industry is a good strategy in trying to ensure seed availability, as the use of seeds saved from previous harvest and borrowing among other farmers are common informal systems used by farmers.

With these in mind, the policy maps out strategies to achieve them. For example, the government will continue its involvement in crop research, focusing more on strategic and long term research which takes care of the traditional and minor crops that are important for household food security amongst small scale farmers and vulnerable communities, including research deemed not attractive to the private sector. Given that small scale farmers would opt for low cost seed varieties, they are likely to find private sector introduced seed varieties costly for any positive return;

hence the continued involvement of government in crop research is welcome.

However, although it would continue to be involved, the policy also provides that government would support private research development by maintaining variety purity on cost recovery basis. In addition, the government would promote the development of the informal sector by providing breeders/basic seed to those that may have no capacity to develop them on cost recovery basis.

On realising that most farmers and seed users might lack the relevant scientific information, government would strengthen the area of information gathering and dissemination through publications to improve access to relevant scientific information and technologies by end – users and researchers. This is critical since improved seed varieties could be underutilised, especially by small scale farmers due to lack of knowledge of their availability.

The success of the seed sector is also heavily dependent on the participation of the private sector. Thus the availability of the seed policy to create the necessary environment for private sector participation is important. In that regard, the policy provides that government will promote the participation of private sector in research through the provision of full access to available germplasm accessions for different crops. The government would also encourage private sector participation in applied research, crop improvement and variety development.

The policy also provides for the protection of farmers from fake seed varieties as well as insufficiently tested varieties. Thus the formalisation of a Variety Release Committee which would provide for wider stakeholder participation is provided for. In addition, a list of seed varieties, which would be updated annually, would be maintained by the government to protect farmers. A National Seeds Committee, to be responsible for monitoring the overall development and function of the seed industry, advise government on policy matters pertaining to the seed industry and review the seed policy and promote national capacity in all areas of the seed industry.

In order to promote entrepreneurship in the seed industry, government would also encourage the establishment of small seed enterprises. However, measures to monitor the informal systems, which include a forum for the coordination of the NGOs operating in the informal seed system, would be put in place to ensure that the activities of the seed entrepreneurs to ensure that their activities create a sustainable cottage seed industry. Most importantly, the policy recognises that the growth and performance of the seed industry would greatly depend on the level of infrastructure development; hence infrastructure in the rural areas, especially roads would be developed to encourage and promote agriculture.

3.1.4 National Cooperative Development Policy (2011)

The formation of cooperative can be a critical strategy, as through this, small scale producers in the agriculture sector could be transformed. The establishment of the following types of service cooperatives for example, which are identified under the policy, might go a long way in helping small scale farmers across the marketing chain:

- Marketing and Supply Co-operatives, which are co-operatives that sell crops produced by the members. These are critical as they would increase the bargaining power of the farmers, compared to a situation where each farmer would sell individually and be at the mercy of middlemen that can easily exploit them.

> The success of the seed sector is also heavily dependent on the participation of the private sector

- Transport Co-operatives, which would be co-operatives running transport facilities for transporting members' produce. Given the poor infrastructure networks, farmers often face challenges in transporting their produce, and are forced to part with significant amount of money as transport costs. Utilising transport from co-operatives would significantly eliminate costs due to the mutual understanding among farmers as well as the eliminated middlemen charges which often inflate the costs.

- Savings and Credit Co-operatives, where members pool their savings and make loans to each other. Given the need for some level of investment into agriculture, farmers should have access to credit to finance agricultural activities. Many farmers often fail to produce on a large scale due to inability to meet some costs related to agriculture inputs. Thus these cooperatives would go a long way in ensuring easy access to cheaper lines of credit for farmers.

This makes it important that strategies be developed to encourage the formation of cooperatives as well as regulating their operations. The Ministry of Agriculture and Livestock thus established the National Cooperative Development Policy in November 2011 with the overall objective of creating an enabling institutional and legal environment for the development of autonomous, transparent, viable and demand – driven co – operatives that contribute to socio – economic development and poverty reduction. This would be achieved through the attainment of the following intermediate objectives:

• To create a framework for reforming and re – orienting the co – operative movement in the context of national development;

• To facilitate the promotion of demand driven, member led, autonomous, viable and sustainable co – operatives;

• To promote the diversification of co – operative activities;

• To create a conducive environment for creation of an effective co – operative structure;

• To provide a framework for efficient resource mobilisation to enhance co – operative development;

• To promote internal and external linkages, and collaboration in service delivery;

• To encourage the formation of other types of co – operatives besides agricultural oriented cooperatives;

Among the identified strategies to achieve these objectives is the development of a legal and institutional framework to facilitate the re – orientation and reforming of the co-operative organisation. This is based on the realisation that the current legislative framework in hardly suitable for the promotion of cooperatives. In addition, the policy hopes to ensure that the Ministry responsible for cooperatives has a physical presence in all the districts of the country through field staff directly dealing with co-operative matters. This would help in strengthening the operations of the cooperatives through regulation.

Given the need to observe international best practice in their conduct, the policy also provides for the development of education and training programmes and materials that address the felt needs of co-operative members and meet the current socio-economic environment. Closely related to this is the need to promote the formation of pre-co-operative groups to adequately prepare co-operators for operational success of cooperatives.

The National Cooperative Development Policy, just like the other agriculture related policies, has also introduced critical strategies that would ensure the development of the agriculture sector. Thus it is generally the extent to which the Ministry of Agriculture and Livestock will go in implementing the identified strategies that would determine the success of the policies.

3.2 Institutional framework

By assessing the various functions that are performed in the agriculture sector, it is easy to identify the key institutions that have to play a positive role to ensure that the Zambia agriculture sector develops. While the Ministry of Agriculture and Livestock (MAL) is the implementing agency for the policies identified in section 3.1, many other institutions are needed to complement government efforts. One of the functions is the provision of agriculture extension services. Although it is generally the Ministry of Agriculture and Co-operatives that provide extension and information through its network at national, provincial and district levels, farmer organizations, the private sector, NGOs and Community Based Organizations (CBOs) also chip in with extension services to farmers.

The other critical function that has to be done in the agriculture sector is the provision of quality seeds to farmers. Institutions that have to complement MAL include theSeed Control and Certification Institute (SCCI), which is responsible for quality control, monitoring seed trade and providing coordination of the sector. The National Plant Genetic Resource Centre also has to come in for collection and preservation of genetic resources, while other research institutions are also responsible for variety development and improvement. Private seed companies, NGOs and CBOs are also heavily involved as they are responsible for production, marketing and distribution of seed.

Ensuring that the soil on which farmers plough and plant crops is suitable is also a critical function for the attainment of agriculture sector objectives. Institutions with a role to play include the Soil and Crops Research Branch of the MAL, which conducts soils and crops research on the basis of crop comparative advantage in line with agro – ecological regions. Other key players in crops research in Zambia are Research Trusts, the University of Zambia, the Ministry of Science, Technology and Vocational Training through the National Science and Technology Council (NSTC) and the National Institute of Scientific and Industrial Research (NISIR) and seed companies.

> The overall objective of this policy is to create an enabling institutional and legal environment for the development of autonomous, transparent, viable and demand-driven co-operatives that contribute to socio-economic development and poverty reduction

Although the Technical Services Branch (TSB) of MAL spearheads irrigation development, the Ministry of Energy and Water Development and theZambia Environmental Management Agency (ZEMA) also have to be involved in the process. The same pattern is also evident with regards to the provision of land husbandry services; although the TSB spearheads this, the Ministry of Lands, Ministry of Works and Supply and the Ministry of Tourism, Environment and Natural Resources, including the Zambia Environmental Management Agency (ZEMA)) also have to be involved.

Training in agriculture is also one of the most important functions that ensure increased productivity. This is offered at various institutions namely the University of Zambia (degree level), Natural Resources Development College (diploma level), Mpika and Monze Agricultural Colleges (certificate). Veterinary training is provided at the University of Zambia (degree level) and the Zambia Institute of Animal Health (certificate level). Others are Kalulushi, Chapula and Kasaka Farm Training Institutes, Palabana Livestock Development Trust and Farm Training Centres; which also provide short-term, demand driven courses. Co-operatives education and training is provided at the Co-operative College, Katete Centre of Marketing and Co-operatives and Kabulamwanda Co-operative Training Centre.

These institutions generally form the key players in ensuring that agriculture development objectives identified under the various agriculture oriented policies are met. Thus their capacity to deliver is also important in meeting the objectives.

3.3 Implementation strategies

In achieving the above objectives the Ministry of Agriculture and Livestock have several activities and programmes. Among these programmes, the following receive much support:

Farmer Input Support Programme (FISP)

It is a well known fact that credit in Zambia is acknowledged to be in short supply, and it is often very costly when available. Since 2002, the government through MAL has attempted to fill the vacuum of lack of access by providing input credit to farmers, (Saasa & Farrington, 2002). Under FISP, the Government has been providing fertilizer and improved seeds to many vulnerable but viable smallholders.

The aim of this programme was to increase agricultural productivity, rural income, food security and help develop the input markets. So far this subsidy has contributed positive result with regards to increased maize production in the country. However it has very little impact on agricultural productivity and poverty reduction (ACF, 2012). In addition to this, the Agriculture Consultative Forum (ACF) findings indicated that the current approach of implementing the FISP is embedded with a lot of challenges such as; high cost to government treasury, poor targeting of intended farmers, delay in delivery of inputs, poor utilization of inputs, crowding out of the private Sector, stifling provision of extension officers and inhibiting of agriculture diversification

FRA – National Strategic Grain Reserves

The Zambian government under the Movement for Multi Party Democracy regime established the Food Reserve Agency (FRA) with the sole purpose of guaranteeing that sufficient maize is always available within national borders to assure food security.

This agency was created as an instrument for assuring food security in the country not as a means for maize market management. Saasa and Farrington's report of 2002 indicated that the main function of the agency was to make good national shortfalls in the availability of maize that was expected to result from an inability on the part of theby then newly emergent private sector to supply the market fully. It is undeniable that this agency that was created for the sole purpose of food reserve is now being used as an instrument for market management. The perceived danger of the FRA engaging in marketing is that it crowds out prospective investment which is a necessary for enhancing market opportunities for small scale farmers as well as providing the needed, efficient backward and forward linkages in the system.

Critics observe that the existence of the FRA deters the development of the private trade, throughthe interactions of millers, famers and brokers or famers accessing the available market access opportunities domestically or internationally. The trail of these critics stems as for as 2000. Saasa & Farrington in 2002 argued that if the private sector was left alone to operate in a free market economy with government only providing the regulatory oversight, would have the incentive, and probably the capacity.

Food Security Pack

In complementing MAL's programmes, the Ministry of Community Development and Social Services instituted this programme 2000 with the vision to empower the vulnerable but yet viable farmers who lost productive assets because of adverse weather condition and the farmers who suffered the negative impact of the Structural Adjustment Reforms that reduced their access to inputs and services.

Initially this programme was a livelihoods development strategy to shift farmers from subsistence to surplus production, and without any doubt this programme has become a core part of Zambia's social safety net. Under the programme, the government provides inputs (seed and fertilizer) to the poor household with the main objective of empowering the targeted households to be self sustained though improved productivity and household food security.

In addition to this, Saasa and Farrington's report of 2002 acknowledges that this programme is now a Social Safety NetProgramme whose main thrust is to improve household food security of vulnerable households by providing them with the means of economic growth and poverty reduction.

Agriculture investment

According to the OECD Investment Policy Reviews of Zambia 2012, the comprehensiveness of investment policies directly impacts on the level of investment, including both local and foreign investment. Transparency, property protection and non discrimination are critical investment policy principles that create a sound investment climate.

As pointed out under the National Agriculture Policy, the MAL would lobby the Ministry of Finance and National Planning and other stakeholders for budgetary provisions of incentives for agriculture investment such as tax breaks and agricultural import/export incentives. The Ministry would also play a role of a marketing agency in linking up potential agricultural investors with the Zambia Investment Centre and help in dissemination of information on investment opportunities and incentives.

The Agricultural Commercialization Program (ACP, 2001) and the National Agricultural and Cooperative Policy (2004) call for the development of an efficient, competitive and sustainable agricultural sector. They see development of infrastructure in high potential agricultural areas and strengthening cooperatives and farmer organisations as a vehicle for achieving this goal (Zambia Investment Report, 2011).

4 Agriculture investment

The Zambian government has thus gone a long way in creating the necessary environment for agriculture investment. One such example is the 'farm block' initiative introduced in 2002, intended to commercialize agricultural land, open up rural areas and attract investors (Nolte K, 2012). As reflected on the Zambia Development Agency (ZDA) website, the development and commercialization of eight farm blocks has already been initiated, intended to make land available for large scale investment to the private sector. The whole Farm Block is expected to be about 100,000 hectares in size, with private sector investors being expected to commercial farms by putting up appropriate infrastructure that will support their agro – business activities. This is expected to help the development of the small, medium and large scale farmers through out – grower schemes for cash – generating agriculture activities for both local and international market. This thus involves land being transformed from customary land to state land, with the government setting up infrastructure services.

According to Zambia investor guide of 2012, the Zambian government has put in place several incentives to encourage investment in the agriculture sector and these incentives are as follows:

- Guaranteed input tax claim for four years prior to commencement of production for agricultural businesses.
- Zero rating agricultural products and supplies when exported.
- VAT deferment on importation some agricultural equipment and machinery.
- Income tax rate of 10 percent.
- Farm improvement allowance at 100 percent on fencing, brick or stone wall and an allowance of K10 million for farm occupied by farm workers.
- Farm works allowance at 100 percent for the full cost of stumping and clearing, works for prevention of soil erosion, boreholes, wells, aerial and geophysical surveys and water conservation.
- Dividends paid out of farming profit are exempt from tax for the first five

years the distributing company commences farming.

- Development allowance is given for any person who incurs expenditure on the growing of tea, coffee or banana plants or citrus trees or similar plants or trees. An allowance of 10 percent of such expenditure shall be deducted in ascertaining the gains and profits of that business.

- No Import Duty on irrigation equipment and reduced Duty Rates on imports of other farming equipment.

- Reduced Customs Duty at 5 percent on pre – mixes, being vitamin additives for animal feed.

Despite of having these incentives, small scale farmers are still not up to date with regard to technologies that facilitate increased productivity of their produce. It goes without saying that small holder farmers are dependent on their ability to produce sufficient amounts of food crops on their farms for their consumption using the conventional way of farming.

According to the crop forecasting survey of 2011/2012, most crops that are grown by small scale farmers have low profit return like maize, millet and cotton as compared as to soya beans and wheat which are highly dominated by the commercial farmers. Commercial farmers accounting for 100 percent production of wheat and 93 percent of soya beans production, these crops have favorable prices and market. It is clear that the Zambian small scale farmers are unable to produce winter wheat because of lack irrigation technology capacity (winter wheat depends solely on irrigation). With regards to soybeans, it being a non tradition crop, there is need of intensive sensitization on how it can be grown and the available markets that exist for this product.

The CFS 2011/2012, indicate that small scale farmers are faced with low productivity levels for their produce. According to Chishala (2007), agricultural productivity among small scale farmers can go up if they are empowered with information and resources to operate efficiently in their production. One evident factor that has affected this productivity is low technology development coming from the government research institutions which are not well funded hence impacting negatively on the small scale farmers. This calls for investment into the sector.

There are different ways through which investors can acquire land in Zambia, depending on whether the land is state land or customary land (Nolte K, 2012). For state land, they can contact ZDA, which would guide the investors by pointing out available land that is ready for investment. In addition, potential investors can also approach existing owners of state land and negotiate on commercial basis for the transfer of the land. Investors can also end up owning customary land by approaching village headmen and chiefs directly in searching for land. However, customary land has to be converted into state land first before it is acquired, and it is this process that might not necessarily observe the PRAI principles.

A case study of the Chiansi irrigation project, located in the Kafue district of Zambia, adjacent to the Kafue River can also be used to assess the nature of investment in Zambia. In 2012, CUTS carried out a study of the scheme, which involved some in-depth interviews with the beneficiary farmers. The findings would be used to assess whether the project carefully observed the PRAI principles. This project, led by InfraCo Limited, is expected to see a sum of U$29 million being injected, with the Dutch government granting $10.5 million.

It is also important to highlight that the project has resulted in some benefits, which could even outweigh the negative issues on investment. The cooperative now holds a 25 percent stake in FarmCo and dividends have been settled at a consistent amount of K250,000 to the locals in order to provide predictability. The purpose of this section is to assess the extent to which the investment framework is in line with the PRAI.

As already mentioned the PRAI framework has seven principles and while principles 5 and 6 have been found to be observed in agriculture investment, there are some grey areas with regards to the following principles, which might call for refinements to the manner in which investment is handled:

- Principle 1: *Existing rights to land and associated natural resources are recognized and respected.*

Among other issues, investment that recognises this principle has to identify all rights holders and negotiate with land holders/users, based on informed and free choice, in order to identify the types of rights to be transferred and modalities for doing so.

The process through which customary land is acquired by investors is often subject to abuse. The chief or the headman is expected to verify first that the land is available and no one claims it, before the writing a letter to the district council, which is also expected to check whether there are any conflicting claims before land is surveyed and used. Although most of the land is often reported to be available when investors come, it is often the case that some dissenting voice would be suppressed first by the chief, especially since it is only the chief and the investor who have to negotiate on a price.

Prior to the installation of the Chiansi irrigation system, there were twenty one families that occupied most part of the fertile land which was used for various livelihood activities that include, among others, crop production, livestock rearing, and brick making for construction of utility shelters. Although twenty of these families were relocated within Chiansi area and became members of the Chanyanya cooperative, one farmer refused to join. The reason for lack of buy – in the project included lack of clarity of the project outputs and how the dividends from the commercial farms will be shared among the farmers. At the time of this research, less than 10 small holder farmers had occupied and fullyutilising the 20 percent land from the 125 members of the cooperative. This appears to suggest that full information was not disclosed to the farmers when land was being acquired; hence the existing rights to land were not fully respected.

It also turned out that about 126 people were permanently removed from their homes and land as it was donated towards the running of the project. The erection of the project meant that indigenous people's shelter, land for keeping livestock and farming land was to be disrupted. Some of the households lost their land against their will. Their relocation on pieces of land smaller than the previous land size has bred some disputes within theneighbourhood especially those with livestock because the animals invade the land in the neighbourhood owing to the fact that there is no leeway for the animals to move freely.

- Principle 2: *Investments do not jeopardize food security but rather strengthen it.*

The Chiansi investment project has even generated regret from some members of the Chanyanya Cooperative. The investment has deprived some indigenous people from growing maize in large volumes since the land that they were relocated to is small in radius and to some extent less fertile compared to that which was contributed towards the project. This according to some respondents has ignited hunger to their households. A visibly annoyed resident lamented that she would not have managed to take her children to school if the project was introduced during the time when her children were still in school; as she was able to raise more money after cultivating on the lager land mass she earlier occupied.

Although meetings on relocation modalities were held and some households concerned consented to the relocation process, the previous location is considered much more fertile compared to the new location. This has hampered productivity among some people as they are unable to cultivate maize for food as well as economic gain.

Besides the Chiansi project, it is also felt that small – scale farmers in general do not see the benefits of the large – scale investments in agriculture sector in Zambia. Their productivity has not changed – but they complain that prices for agricultural products have fallen due to the large scale production of the commercial farms. This endangers the livelihoods of net sellers of agricultural products (Arslan Aslihan *et al*, 2011).

- Principle 3: *Processes relating to investment in agriculture are transparent, monitored, and ensure accountability by all stakeholders, within a proper business, legal, and regulatory environment.*

There are general feelings that transparency might be lacking on the Chiansi project as there has been a lack of consistency on the data provided by InfraCo on the amount of land involved in the Chanyanya pilot project. The Chiansi Irrigation Briefing paper prepared by InfraCo in March 2010; the InfraCo official project webpage and the InfraCo documentary on the Chanyanya project contain inconsistent information regarding the breakdown on how land is distributed in the project.

- Principle 4: *All those materially affected are consulted, and agreements from consultations are recorded and enforced.*

This requires clarity on: a) procedural requirements b) the character of agreements reached in such consultations and c) how the agreements can be enforced. Given that the land involved would be owned by different households, it is difficult for all involved to reach an agreement with the investor under the same terms and conditions. The voices of dissent among some completed project point to the fact that agreements were not necessarily reached with all those affected before such investments were effected; hence this principle was not adequately observed.

- Principle 7: *Environmental impacts of a project are quantified and measures taken to encourage sustainable resource use, while minimizing the risk/magnitude of negative impacts and mitigating them.*

There are general concerns that regulations on environment are often evaded. In Zambia, large – scale investors must provide an environmental impact assessment to the Zambia Environmental Management Agency (ZEMA) at time of purchase, but often this is not done. Many investors start production without contacting the ZEMA, despite the existence of the regulation (Arslan Aslihan et al, 2011).

5

Fieldwork findings

In order to get an understanding about the challenges facing farmers, a sample of 120 farmers were interviewed to gather their views and experiences. Among these, 40 farmers were from the Copperbelt Province, 40 were from the Eastern Province while 40 were from the Southern Province. In addition, other stakeholders interviewed were District Agricultural Coordinators' offices, Agricultural Consultative Forum, Livestock Development Trust, Indaba agricultural Policy Research Institute, ZNFU, Beef Association of Zambia, ZDA and Cotton Association of Zambia.

5.1　Input side

5.1.1　Access to Land

The findings from the interview with farmers indicate that in the rural part of Zambia, small scale farmers rely on traditional land tenure systems in acquiring farm land. In most instances the land is usually held by a group, community lineage or clan, family or individuals. An individual in the community/ village can give a piece of it to another person for use, with the local leaders' knowledge. Once acquired, land may be passed on from generation to generation. In that regard, farmers were also asked about the source of their land ownership (Figure 2).

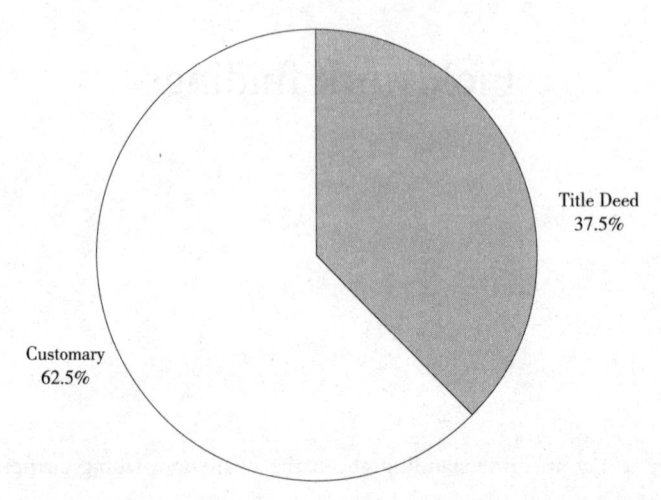

Figure 2　Distribution of Land ownership among interviewed household
Source: Interview results.

In Zambia specifically in the Copperbelt, Eastern and Southern Province, the predominant form of land ownership is customary land ownership. As reflected in our findings, about 62.5 percent of the respondents indicated that they have customary ownership to the land while 37.5 percent indicated that they had title deeds. The Copperbelt Province has however gone a long way in trying to formalise land ownership compared to the other two provinces; most of the farmers who indicated that they had title deeds were from the Copperbelt province. Overall, about 70 percent of the farmers who indicated that they had title deeds were from Copperbelt province, which is not surprising since it is an urban province where some farmers were former mine workers who switched to farming for their livelihood when there was a slowdown in the mining activities and most miners where retrenched.

5.1.2　Access to Irrigation

Improved irrigation system is one of the key drivers of the agriculture sector in any country. In Zambia it is undeniable that the irrigation sector has remained stagnant despite being endowed with enough water resource. Tapping subsurface water is still a pipe dream among most small scale farmers. Being specific, small scale farmers who produce cotton, groundnuts and maize in the Copperbelt, Southern and Eastern province depend on the rains for good yields. In that regard, farmers were also asked whether they have access to irrigation, and the results show that those farmers with access to irrigation do so using the bucket/watering can system (Figure 3).

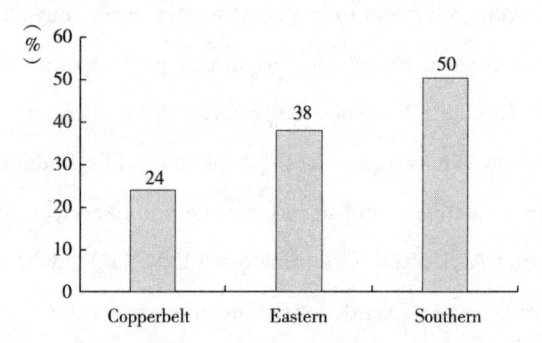

Figure 3 Access to irrigation by using bucket/ watering can
Source: *Interview Result.*

The findings indicate that, with regards to the sample only 24, 38 and 50 percent of farmers had access to irrigation in Copperbelt, Eastern and Southern Province respectively by the usage of watering can, this means that 76, 62 and 50 percent of the farmers had no access to any form of irrigation in Copperbelt, Eastern and Southern Province respectively. Only 1 percent of the small scale farmers were using Treddle pumps in southern province to irrigate their farms. This form of irrigation is specifically for their horticultural crops, thus these farmers do not use any form of irrigation for the cotton, groundnuts and maize crops. This is also consistent with findings from other studies, where it was established that despite Zambia being in possession of over 423, 000 hectare of irrigable land, only 0.9 percent of its arable is irrigated (ECI*Africa*, 2012). This shows the need to come up with intervention that can stimulate investment with regards to irrigation of field and cash crops.

5.1.3　Access to Extension/ Inputs

The provision of extension services to the farming population through the extension workers ofMinistry of Agriculture and Livestock (MAL) is an important responsibility of the government. The effectiveness of government in providing this vital service depends on trained personnel and the number of farmers they are covering. In Copperbelt, Eastern and Southern province, on average 1 extension officer covers 1000 farmers. On average farmers indicated that they were only visited by extension officers three times in a year. About 71, 78 and 84 percent of the farmers in Copperbelt, Eastern and Southern Province respectively who were interviewed indicated that they had access to extension services (Table 5). The findings indicate that distance has an effect in delivery and access of extension services. This was also confirmed by the District Agriculture Coordinators (DACOs), who indicated that they are very under-staffed with regards extension officers.

All the farmers who were interviewed mentioned that they were not satisfied with the level of their access to extension services.

Table 5　Distribution of Households by Access and Proximity to Extension Services

Area (Provinces)	No of H/Hs Surveyed	percent of H/Hs accessing extension services	percent of H/Hs accessing extension services by Distance Area	
			Dist ≤5km	Dist >5km
Copperbelt	40	71	100	74
Eastern	40	78	100	76
Southern	40	84	100	80

Source: *Interview results.*

Figure 4 amplifies the findings by indicating that distance has an effect on access to extension service; this graph shows that the greater the distance the lesser the chance for small scale farmers to have access to extension services. With regards to Southern Province, there is an indication that there is a decline in terms of the percentage of farmers having access extension services from 100 to 85 and then to 75 percent for farmers within the proximity of 0 – 5 km, 5 – 10 km and greater than 10 km respectively and this decline applies to other provinces as it can be seen in the graph

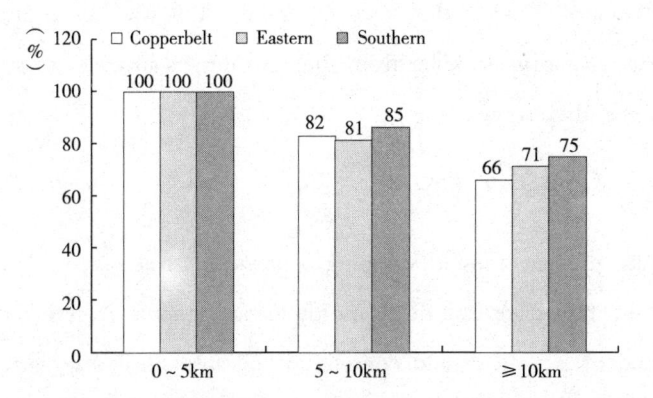

Figure 4 Percentage of Household having access to extension services by distance
Source: *Interview results.*

Input access was analyzed by looking at cotton, groundnuts and maize separately for the crops and beef and goat production separately for livestock.

Starting with the livestock, with regards to goat production, all the farmers indicated that they use free scavenging methods to feed the goats. With regards to beef production, the herd cattle are normally taken to feed on maize stover during the dry season and available pastures. In rain season, there is enough grazing pasture for beef animals. Thus almost all the farmers interviewed generally do not purchase any inputs into livestock farming, being heavily reliant on nature.

In cotton farming, the findings indicate that all interviewed farmers receive inputs throughout – grower schemes offered by the ginnery companies. The Ministry of Agriculture and Livestock indicated that the cotton sector is characterized by effective provision of inputs and extension services by the Ginners. These ginnery companies offer the right amount of inputs and the right time to their farmers at a credit. They also provide extension and marketing services.

The groundnuts farmers who were interviewed indicated that they use recycled seed and are very reluctant in adopting new and improved varieties. On maize farming, 98 percent of the farmers interviewed indicated that they receive inputs through the Farmers Input Support Programme, although 70 percent of these farmers indicated that the amount of input they received under FISP was not enough and hence they buy fertilizer and weed killer from the agro dealers in order to supplement the subsidized inputs they receive.

5. 1. 4 Access to Credit

In Zambia just like most developing countries, farmers generally lack cash resources to meet immediate cash needs mostly for farm inputs. Access to credit from financial institutions is difficult and complicated because small scale farmers lack adequate collateral security. Credit among farmers is acknowledged to be in short supply; it is often very costly when available. The government of Zambia attempt to fill the vacuum of lack of access by providing subsidized inputs to farmers. Some small scale farmers occasionally receive input credit from private companies for the cultivation of cash crops such as cotton.

All the farmers who were interviewed indicated that they lack access to credit schemes offered by financial institution; this can be attributed to the fact that the cost of borrowing in Zambia is high and not favourable to the small scale farmers.

FAO report of 2008 amplifies our findings in that credit for livestock production activities for smallholder farmers is almost non – existent in the country. There has been a gap in the provision of financial services in the rural areas. This followed the collapse of most of the subsidized and publicly funded rural finance institutions in the mid – 1990s.

This partial and often complete lack of access to rural financial services hinders smallholder's efforts to improve, expand and diversify their farm activities so as to earn enough income to improve their livelihood. The challenge thus remains to find solutions to the problem of access to credit by small – scale farmers who lack collateral assets. Many institutional innovations have been introduced in recent years to solve this problem but these have not performed very well.

5.1.5 Access to Veterinary Services

The veterinary services in Zambia still leave a lot to be desired. Access to veterinary services is often looked at as a measure of the policy intent to agricultural development especially in rural areas where communities are major livestock producers (Kalinda et al, 2008). In this regard, farmers were also asked about access and proximity to veterinary services (Table6).

Table 6 Distribution of Households by Access and Proximity to Veterinary Services

Area (Provinces)	No of H/Hs Surveyed	Percentage of H/Hs Accessing Veterinary services	Percentage of H/Hs accessing veterinary services by Distance Area	
			Dist ≤5km	Dist >5km
Copperbelt	40	67	100	63
Eastern	40	78	100	75
Southern	40	82	100	81

Source: *Interview results.*

The research results show that access is quite low in Copperbelt as compared to Eastern province and Southern province as 67, 78 and 82 percent of the farmers in Copperbelt, Eastern and Southern province respectively had access to veterinary services. It was also discovered that access to drugs by farmers depends on farmers having capacity to buy drugs and call for the services of the District Veterinary Officer's office to assist in administering these drugs. However some of the farmers have received some training in administering these drugs. The government services normally comes in during emergency, for instance when there is an outbreak of a disease like corridor, foot and mouth etc. The artificial insemination and dip tank services are not well developed in these provinces and dip tanks which exist are in deplorable state.

Statistics indicate that there has been inadequate resource allocation towards veterinary services; this is one of the major limits to improving and increasing agricultural production and reducing poverty. Only about 6 percent of the national budget has been devoted to the agriculture sector in the past three years thereby limiting the amount that is allocated to livestock disease control programmes. The cut in government expenditure has had a direct consequence on the quality and coverage of government agricultural services like extension. The situation might be worsening if one looked at the 2013 budget allocation where the percentage has been reduced from about 6.3 percent to 5.7 percent.

This in turn has a negative effect on the productivity in the agricultural sector as a whole. Further, before the liberalization of the economy, some extension activities such as those involving veterinary services had functioned effectively. These have been almost entirely discontinued in most rural communities due to lack of funding. As a result, farmers raising cattle have been losing many animals to corridor disease and other livestock diseases. In places like the Southern Province, the heavy losses of oxen have had a major impact on both cash and food crop production and thus negatively affecting their livelihoods. In addition, only limited credit facilities exist for livestock producers, traders and processors (Kalinda et al, 2008).

Figure 5 belowamplifies on the findings and showcases that distance has an effect on access to veterinary service. This figure shows that the greater the distance the lesser percentage of small scale farmers have access to extension services. On Copperbelt province, there was an indication that there is a decline in terms of the percentage of farmers having access extension services from 100 to 80 and then to 66 percent for farmers within the proximity of 0 – 5 km, 5 – 10 km and greater than 10 km respectively and this decline applies to other provinces as it can be seen in the graph.

5.1.6 Access to Closest Permanent Road

In Zambia, most farmers in rural areas face difficulties in finding markets be-

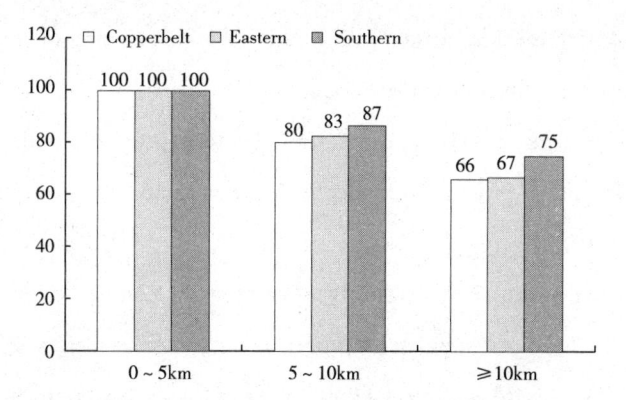

Figure 5 Percentage of Household having access to Veterinary Services by distance

Source: *Interview results.*

cause of the terrain they live in and lack of permanent and well maintained roads. It goes without saying that farm households need social and infrastructure support to effectively attain a better standardof living. In addition, social and infrastructure support include (a) access to input and output markets, (b) access to health centres and schools, and (c) participation in governmental and NGO support programs (Kalinda et al, 2008). It is very evident that the condition of the roads in most of the rural areas which were visited are usually seasonal gravel roads which are rarely maintained and lack permanent transportation services. Nevertheless, one could occasionally spot itinerant traders roaming the villages to buy grains from the farmers in the rural districts.

All the farmersthat were interviewed mentioned that they had access to roads but expressed concern on the state of roads which they said were in a deplorable state. The resultant effect of the state of this is an increase the cost of transportation and hence leading to increased cost of production and marketing.

5.2 Output side

Most of the Zambian Farmers are involved in maize crop production because they have a readily available market with a favourable price being offered by the Food Reserve Agency. Southern province produces more maize than Copperbelt and Eastern province. In terms of the expected sales, eastern province under performed as compared to the other province. Copperbelt's productivity was better than the other provinces.

Overall, the productivity levelon various crops in Zambia still leaves a lot to be desired. There is need to integrate appropriate technologies that will enhance crop productivity. With regards to productivity (Yield/ha), Copperbelt is performing better than the Eastern and Southern province hence the need to assess the scope of replicating the practices being implored Copperbelt to improve the productivity of the other provinces. Eastern province performed better in cotton and groundnuts production compared to Copperbelt and Eastern province (Table 7).

Table 7 2011/2012 Crop Forecasting Survey

Crop	Province	Area Planted (Ha)	Area Harvested (Ha)	Expected Production (MT)	Yield (MT/Ha)	Expected Sales (MT)
Maize	Copperbelt	89501	79329	205542	2.30	122306
	Eastern	276288	245319	572760	2.07	214265
	Southern	303429	227076	554275	1.83	257126
Groundnuts	Copperbelt	8709	8447	5399	0.62	2892
	Eastern	56903	54793	30895	0.54	10223
	Southern	22874	20420	9514	0.42	2.040
Cotton	Copperbelt	605	605	785	1.30	—
	Eastern	190607	184472	160956	0.84	—
	Southern	40380	36460	33417	0.83	—

Source: *Crop Forecast Survey*, 2011/2012.

According to theZambia Central Statistics Office, by 2010 cattle population was 3038000 and goat population was 758501 in the country. It is undeniable that goats are second from pigs in terms of their prolific value. There is need to look at goat production from commercialization side, as this is a product that has a huge and specialised export market through Kasumbalesa and Nakonde border posts. Existing literature reveals that an increasing demand for livestock products such goat meat can offer small – scale farmers opportunities for increased market participation. However, the literature also highlights that existing goat markets are largely informal, with poorly developed inputs and services.

Coming to storage facilities in these provinces (Copperbelt, Eastern and Southern), the findings reveals that storage facilities being used by farmers are not well developed and this has led to the increases in the post harvest losses being incurred by farmers. The farmers who have traditional storage facilities indicated that they have challenges on pest control related issues, stacking, record keeping and fire safety arrangements and above all limited storage space.

And on the livestock sector, the farmers indicated that the cold storage facilities among small scale farmers are in non existence. This has hindered the small scale farmers in ensuring continuous production of goat meat and beef production.

5.3 Marketing issues

Starting with maize, the biggest market player is the government through FRA; all the famers indicated that they were not satisfied with the operations of FRA because the agency delays to buy their produce and delays to pay them on time; hence hindering them from effective planning for thesubsequent seasons. The government of Zambia through the MAL determines the floor price of maize which is currently K65000 per 50kg of maize. This crop has attracted a lot of farmers in its production because of the readily available market offering a better price and by the nature of it being a staple crop for Zambia. Despite this attractive price, all the farmers indicated that they face delay in purchasing and payment by FRA thereby leaving them without any alternative but turn to briefcase business men who offer them very prices averaging K40000, which is much lower than the floor price.

There is also a positive side. Due to the enabling environment created by the government in the maize sector, it has attracted most of the small scale farmers and this can be attested to the fact that all the farmers who were interviewed are involved in maize farming despite other farming activities. The conducive marketing environment that has been created has crowded out investment in the other crop sectors as this can be reaffirmed by a continuous decline in the diversification index (Table 8).

Table 8　Crop Diversification Index

Area	2005/2006	2006/2007	2007/2008	2008/2009	2009/2010	2010/2011
Other major crops (Ha)	949037	943355	902493	1119465	1133808	1093090
Maize crop (Ha)	784524	872812	928224	1125466	1242271	1355764
Diversification Index	1.21	1.08	0.97	0.99	0.91	0.81

Source: ACF, 2012.

Thediversification index is calculated by the area planted to other crops divided by area planted by maize. Hence the table show increased concentration towards maize.

The cotton sector is under the control of the private sector. All the farmers who were interviewed indicated that they are under out grower schemes and are liable to sell their produce to respective ginneries that pre – financed their production. The ginneries (Dunavant, Cargill and Alliance) are the key players in this sector as they contract farmers through out – grower scheme to produce cotton. Under this out – grower scheme, farmers are given inputs at a credit and extension services. This credit is normally considered during the setting of the market price. The market price of cotton depends on the international market, whenever the international market prices have gone down, farmers are informed of the trend but when the price is up, these companies are reluctant to inform the farmers of the good prevailing international market; hence making supernormal profit at the expense of the small scale farmers. This lack of transparency in this sector has led to most farmers stopping producing cotton.

The groundnut sector's marketing channels are not well developed, this market is quite informal. Farmers produce and sell to fellow farmers producing other crops and this crop fetches a higher price on the market. The market for this crop is readily available.

Our findings indicate that the women arelargely responsible for the planting, weeding, and harvesting of groundnuts. In terms of marketing, women tend to dominate the small – scale informal groundnut trade in rural and urban markets. Our findings also indicated that 75 percent of the female headed households in Copperbelt, Eastern and Southern Province were involved in groundnuts production and marketing.

The problem in this sector is that farmers are unable to sort groundnuts according to varieties and grades, if they had this capacity they would have been able to maximize their returns. There is also a problem with post harvest handling of groundnuts by these farmers which increases the level of *aflatoxin* in groundnuts hence preventing the crop from meeting international standards. There is need to deal with *aflatoxin* by investing in technologies that can reduce its incidences, e. g. invest in cocoons and improved sacks (FSRP, 2012).

The farmers indicated that beef has a good market though 95 percent of them indicated that they inherited and keep cattle for prestige purpose and only sell when great need arises. Farmers in this sector should be sensitized on the importance of commercialization. The same is true for farmers in the goat sector, who keep goats not for business but for family events and only sell when need arises.

6

Conclusions and recommendations

What is quite apparent from the study is that there is still a lot of scope for the agriculture sector to improve, especially if more attention is devoted to the small scale farmers. They account for more than 70 percent of the farmers and dominate the farming of maize, millet, sorghum, groundnuts and cotton. The study has identified some issues that need urgent attention to ensure that small scale farmers' productivity is enhanced. For instance, access to irrigation is poor; this can be attested by the use of buckets and watering can system by small scale farmers. Productivity of their produce can be increased if farmers use alternative sources of irrigation such as installation of pumps, have provisions of harvesting rain water and its storage.

The National Agriculture Policy provides that there would be regularisation of the seed sector through seed testing, seed crop inspection, variety registration, variety protection and enforcement of seed quality standards to facilitate seed trade, quarantine and other seed related issues. Although cotton farmers indicated that they receive quality seeds through out – grower schemes offered by the ginnery companies, the groundnut sector still has challenges. The groundnuts farmers indicated that they use recycled seeds, largely available from informal sources; hence the policy is not being effectively implemented. Although the NAP provides for the development

6 Conclusions and recommendations

of the informal seed sector by providing accessibility of the sector to breeders/basic seed from research, findings reveal that farmers are unable to sort groundnuts according to varieties and grades due to lack of capacity in sorting techniques. In addition groundnut farmers are reluctant in adopting new and improved varieties – this may be due to information asymmetry and hence the need to organise training programmes at ground level regarding the use of new and improved varieties which will enhance productivity and also improve the delivery of effective extension services. There is also need to open seed banks at provincial level. This is also something that the implementation of the policy would have gone a long way in addressing.

Although farmer groups and farmer field schools and the use of electronic and print media as communication tools to support extension information delivery are strategies identified by the NAP, the implementation is yet to kick off in earnest. As reported in the study, farmers indicated that they were only visited by extension officers three times in a year and only about 71, 78 and 84 percent of the farmers in Copperbelt, Eastern and Southern Province respectively who were interviewed indicated that they had access to extension services. Since the District Agriculture Coordinators confirmed this and attributed it to under – staffing, it is quite apparent that the implementation of the policy needs to be enhanced to increase access to extension services. In order to have an effective and efficient extension service delivery, there is need to build capacity in terms of adequate staffing and operation efficiency, and increasing access to extension services requires the office of the DACOs to open sub branches in every 10 km radius.

The NAP is also yet to deal with the issue of access to finance, despite the fact that the NAP proposes to create a fund for access by farmers through appropriate financial institutions and to encourage group lending. All the farmers who were interviewed indicated that they lack access to credit schemes offered by financial institution; this can be attributed to the fact that the cost of borrowing in Zambia is high and not favourable to the small scale farmers. Thus it is recommended that the government should start to put in place measures that ensure that access to credit by small scale farmers is enhanced, in line with the NAP. The government should promote the provision of Micro finance through cooperative system and encouraging the establishment of self help groups. There is need to encourage contract farming with the private sector while government plays the regulatory role.

In addition, although NAP promises strategies that facilitate market information flow among stakeholders in various regions, including facilitating the provision of rural infrastructure such as roads, rural storage infrastructure and developing market centres, marketing is still a challenge for small scale farmers. The groundnut sector's marketing channels are largely informal. Findings also reveal that in the three provinces, the storage facilities being used by farmers are not well developed, leading to post harvest losses. Challenges with regards to pest control, record keeping and fire safety arrangements etc also compound matters. In the livestock sector, the farmers face challenges due to non – existent cold storage facilities (government should take initiations and encourage private investment to build storage facilities), making it difficult for the small scale farmers to continuously produce goat meat and beef. Thus the provisions on marketing in the NAP call for urgent implementation. In amplifying implementation, there is need to establish provincial call centres/ information cells. There is also need of capacity building workshops to disseminate market information that are arranged by the state and other key stakeholders to disseminate market information.

Implementation gaps are also apparent in the irrigation policy. Although updating the standards and guidelines for the planning, design and construction of irrigation schemes to benefit small scale farmers, this is yet to commence on a large scale. The fact that about 76, 62 and 50 percent of the farmers had no access to any form of irrigation in Copperbelt, Eastern and Southern Province respectively is worrisome. There is need to scale up the implementation of the irrigation policy to enhance agriculture productivity by small scale farmers as mentioned earlier.

6 Conclusions and recommendations

The strategies identified by the National Cooperative Development Policy would also enhance the performance of small scale farmers. The development of a legal and institutional framework to facilitate the re – orientation and reforming of the co – operative organisation and ensuring that the Ministry responsible for cooperatives has a physical presence in all the districts of the country through field staff directly dealing with co – operative matters is provided for. Cooperative farming should be encouraged to ensure productive returns to the farmers. Re – structuring of existing of cooperative organisations are required in terms of its staffing and operational efficiency.

There is also need for a change of attitude if goat production is to be enhanced in Zambia. All the farmers indicated that they use free scavenging methods to feed the goats, with no formalised feeding schemes in place. The same is equally true for beef production, which is largely reliant on traditional pastures as inputs into the farming activity. There is need for orientation of Small scale farmers as well as capacity building support to ensure that the need to treat both goat and beef farming as a business, which would also call for some investments. Government support towards this would also go a long way in enhancing productivity.

The study has also established that although investment into the agriculture sector is welcome there is need to encourage private sector participation for investment in technology. There are also some issues that need attention to ensure that the investment is in line with the PRAI. There is need to ensure that the existing rights to land and associated natural resources are recognized and respected by ensuring that some households do not lose land against their will. There is also need to ensure that full information is disclosed to the farmers when land is being acquired as a way of respecting rights to land. Instances where uptake by the displaced farmers is too low in newly invested areas might imply that the investment is jeopardizing food security as farmers' production would become lower than the situation before the investment. Efforts should also be enhanced to ensure that all those materially affected by the huge investments are consulted, and agreements from consultations are recorded and enforced.

One challenge that is also apparent is the weak land tenure system among the farmers. As found out in the report, the predominant form of land ownership is customary land ownership, with only 37.5 percent of the respondents indicating that they had title deeds. Among these, about 70 percent were from Copperbelt province, an urban province. Having title deeds would go a long way in helping the farmers to unlock credit, as these could be used as collateral. There is need for a relook into the land tenure system to ensure that more farmers have title deeds to their land.

References

- Bwalya, S., H. Haantuba, T. Kalinda and A. Mulolwa (2008), *Use of intergrated Land Use Assessment (ILUA) data for forestry and agricultural policy review and analysis in Zambia*, FAO, 2008.
- Chishala, B. H. (2007), *Analysis of Agricultural Technologies and Dissemination Situation in Zambia*, SADC, 2007.
- CSPR (2010), *Sixth National Development Plan for Zambia, 2011 - 2015: A Civil Society Perspective* (2010), CSPR, 2010.
- CSO (2007), *Zambia Demographic Health Survey* (2007), CSO, 2007.
- Farrington, J. and O. Saasa (2002), *Drivers for change in Zambia Agriculture: Defining what shapes the policy environment*, DFID, 2010.
- MAL (2012), *Crop Forecast Survey 2011/2012*, Ministry of Agriculture and Livestock, 2012.
- MAL (2004), *Irrigation Policy (2004)*, Ministry of Agriculture and Livestock, 2004.
- MAL (2004), *National Agricultural Policy (2004 - 2015)*, Ministry of Agriculture and Livestock, 2004.
- MAL (2012), *National Cooperative Development Policy (2011)*, Ministry of Agriculture and Livestock, 2011.
- MAL (2012), *National Seed Industrial Policy (1999)*, Ministry of Agriculture and Livestock, 1999.
- OECD (2012), *Zambia Investment Policy Review (2012)*, OECD, 2012.
- UNDP (2011), *Zambia Human Development Report (2011)*, UNDP, 2011.

图书在版编目(CIP)数据

赞比亚农业发展及其对小农生计的影响／卢萨卡国际消费者团结与信托协会著；刘海方，田欣，周灿灿译.—北京：社会科学文献出版社，2014.3
 ISBN 978-7-5097-5499-3

Ⅰ.①赞… Ⅱ.①卢…②刘…③田…④周… Ⅲ.①农业经济-经济发展-研究-赞比亚 Ⅳ.①F347.33

中国版本图书馆CIP数据核字（2013）第311225号

赞比亚农业发展及其对小农生计的影响

著　　者／卢萨卡国际消费者团结与信托协会
译　　者／刘海方　田欣　周灿灿

出 版 人／谢寿光
出 版 者／社会科学文献出版社
地　　址／北京市西城区北三环中路甲29号院3号楼华龙大厦
邮政编码／100029

责任部门／全球与地区问题出版中心
　　　　　（010）59367004
电子信箱／bianyibu@ssap.cn
项目统筹／高明秀

责任编辑／高明秀　许玉燕
　　　　　于静静
责任校对／张文飞
责任印制／岳　阳

经　　销／社会科学文献出版社市场营销中心（010）59367081　59367089
读者服务／读者服务中心（010）59367028

印　　装／三河市尚艺印装有限公司
开　　本／787mm×1092mm　1/16　　印　张／7.75
版　　次／2014年3月第1版　　　　　字　数／122千字
印　　次／2014年3月第1次印刷
书　　号／ISBN 978-7-5097-5499-3
定　　价／49.00元

本书如有破损、缺页、装订错误，请与本社读者服务中心联系更换

▲ 版权所有　翻印必究